MICROSOFT OUTLOOK 2022

Complete Beginner to Expert Guide That Teaches Everything You Need to Know About Microsoft Outlook Including Tips & Tricks to Help You Stay Organized and Achieve Maximum Productivity

TABINA HENDRICK

Copyright © 2022 TABINA HENDRICK

All Rights Reserved

This book or parts thereof may not be reproduced in any form, stored in any retrieval system, or transmitted in any form by any means—electronic, mechanical, photocopy, recording, or otherwise—without prior written permission of the publisher, except as provided by United States of America copyright law and fair use.

Disclaimer and Terms of Use

The author and publisher of this book and the accompanying materials have used their best efforts in preparing this book. The author and publisher make no representation or warranties with respect to the accuracy, applicability, fitness, or completeness of the contents of this book. The information contained in this book is strictly for informational purposes. Therefore, if you wish to apply the ideas contained in this book, you are taking full responsibility for your actions.

Printed in the United States of America

CONTENTS

CONTENTS III
INTRODUCTION 1
CHAPTER 1 4
OUTLOOK FEATURES YOU NEED TO KNOW 4

   EXPLAINING WHY SO MANY PEOPLE USE OUTLOOK 4
      Offline access to email messages 4
      A customized mode of organizing email 5
      Grouping email items for better organization 5
      Rules to reduce the clutter of email 6
      Access to rich contact information 6
      Scheduling meetings 6
      The ability to ignore conversations 7
      Sharing and delegating calendars 7
      The Easiest Way to Do Anything in Outlook 8
      Using a focus box 9
      Share Calendars 9
      Make use of the scheduling assistant 10
      Get people's attention by mentioning them 10
      Customizing the swipe options 10
   USING EMAIL: BASIC DELIVERY TECHNIQUES 10
      Initial Setup of an Email Account 11
      Reading email 11
      Answering email 12
      Creating new email messages 13
      Schedule sending mail; send it later. 14
      Forwarding an email message 15
      Sending a File 16
      Maintaining Your Schedule 18
      Opening an appointment in Outlook 19
      Adding a contact 20
      Entering a Task 23
      Taking Notes 24
      Categorizing Outlook notes 26

CHAPTER 2 29
GETTING MORE DONE WITH LESS EFFORT 29

Outlook and Other Programs 29
Postbox 29
Thunderbird 30
Spike 30
Mailbird 31

OUTLOOK'S MAIN SCREEN 31
Using the Folder pane 31

THE INFORMATION VIEWER: OUTLOOK'S HOTSPOT 33
THE RIBBON TIES 35
Viewing Screen Tips 35
Using the New Items Button 35
Finding Things in a Flash with Instant Search 36
Taking Peeks 36
Getting Help in Outlook 37

CHAPTER 3 39
ON THE FAST TRACK: DRAG TILL YOU DROP 39

Dragging 39
Dispatching Tasks in a Flash 40
Making Time Stand Still With Calendar Wizardry 41
Keeping Friends Close and Enemies Closer 42
Creating Instant Email Messages 44
Creating an email from a name in your contact list 44
Outlook Workspace Expansion 45
Changing the font or font size located in the reading pane 47

CHAPTER 4 49
THE ESSENTIAL SECRETS OF EMAIL 49

Front Ends and Back Ends 49
Creating Messages 50
The quick and dirty way 50
The slow and complete way 52
Setting priorities 55
Setting sensitivity 55
Setting other message options 56

Adding an internet link to an email message.. 57
Reading and Replying to Email Messages 57
Viewing previews of message text... 58
Sending a reply.. 60
Resending messages... 61
Don't get caught by phishing 62
THAT'S NOT MY DEPARTMENT: FORWARDING EMAIL 63
Blind Copying for Privacy 64
Deleting Messages 65
Saving Interrupted Messages 66
Saving a Message as a File... 67

CHAPTER 5 70

EMAIL TOOLS YOU CAN'T DO WITHOUT 70

Nagging by Flagging 70
One-click flagging.. 70
Setting flags for different days... 71
Changing the default flag date... 72
Adding a flag with a customized reminder... 72
Changing the date on a reminder 73
Saving Copies of Your Messages 74
Setting Your Reply and Forward Options 75
Adding Comments to a Reply or a Forward 76
Sending Attachments... 77
Emailing Screenshots 80
Creating Signatures for Your Messages 81

CHAPTER 6 84

DEALING WITH MESSAGES... 84

Organizing Folders 84
Creating a new email folder 85
Moving messages to another folder... 85
Organizing Your Email with Search Folders... 86
Setting up a search folder.. 86
Using a search folder 89
Deleting a search folder... 89
Using the Reading Pane 89

v

Playing by the Rules *90*
Creating a rule *91*
Putting a rule into action *94*
Filtering Junk Email *95*
Fine-tuning the filter's sensitivity *96*
Filtering your email with sender and recipient lists *98*
Filtering domains *101*
Archiving for Posterity *101*
Setting up Auto Archive *102*
Setting AutoArchive for individual folders *104*
Starting the archive process manually *106*
Finding and viewing archived items *107*
Closing the archive data file *108*
Arranging Your Messages *109*
Viewing conversations *113*
Ignoring conversations *114*
Cleaning up conversations *115*
Simplifying Tasks Using Quick-Steps *118*
Creating and managing Quick-Steps *121*
Creating Quick Parts to save keystrokes *124*

CHAPTER 7 .... **125**

MANAGING CONTACTS, DATES, TASKS AND MORE **125**

Putting in Your Contacts' Names, Numbers, and Other Stuff *125*
The quick and dirty way to enter contacts. *126*
The slow, complete way to enter contact *126*
Viewing the contacts *130*
View Sorting *131*
Rearranging Views *132*
Using grouped views *132*
Identifying Your Friends *134*
Using Contact Information *135*
Searching for contacts *136*
Finding a contact from any Outlook module *138*
Sending a business card *138*
Gathering people into groups *140*
Creating a Contact Group *140*
Editing a contact group *142*

  Adding pictures to contacts *142*

CHAPTER 8 .... **144**

UNLEASHING THE CALENDAR'S POWER **144**

  Getting Around the Outlook Calendar *144*
  Meetings Galore: Scheduling appointments *146*
  The quick and dirty way to enter an appointment *146*
  The complete way to enter an appointment *147*
  Changing the dates *148*
  Dates are being broken. *151*
  Getting a Good View of Your Calendar *154*
  Printing Your Appointments *155*
  Adding Holidays *156*
  Handling Multiple Calendars *157*
  Creating multiple calendars *157*
  Managing multiple calendars *158*

CHAPTER 9 .... **159**

TASK MASTERY **159**

  Entering New Tasks in the Tasks Module *159*
  The quick-and-dirty way to enter a task *159*
  The regular way to enter a task *160*
  Adding an Internet link to a task *162*
  Editing Your Tasks *163*
  The quick-and-dirty way to change a task *163*
  The regular way to change a task *164*
  Deleting a task *166*
  Managing Recurring Tasks *166*
  Creating a regenerating task *168*
  Skipping a recurring task once *169*
  Marking Tasks as Finished *169*
  Marking it off *170*
  Picking a color for completed or overdue tasks *170*
  View Your Tasks *171*
  Frequenting the To-Do Bar *173*
  Adding a new item to the To-Do bar *174*
  Tasks in the Calendar *174*

CHAPTER 10 176
CUSTOMIZING OUTLOOK 176

Customizing the Quick Access Toolbar 176
Customizing the Ribbon 177
Taking in the Views 178
Table/List view 179
Card view 179
Calendar views 179
Playing with Columns in Table and List Views 180
Adding a column 180
Moving a column 181
Widening or narrowing a column 181
Removing a column 182
Sorting Items 182
Sorting in the Table View 183
Sorting from the Sort dialog box 183
Grouping Items 184
Viewing grouped items 184
Viewing headings only 185
Saving Custom Views 185
Using Categories 186
Assigning a category 186
Renaming a category 187
Changing a category color 187
Assigning a category shortcut key 188

CHAPTER 11 190
SOCIAL MEDIA MAGIC WITH OUTLOOK RSS 190

Brushing Up on Social Media Basics 191
Sending an SOS to RSS 191
Feeling like a social butterfly 192
Podcasts 192
Blogs 193
Subscribing to an RSS Feed via Internet Explorer 193
Setting Up an RSS Feed in Outlook 195
Reading Feeds 197

CHAPTER 12 198

MANAGING MULTIPLE EMAIL ACCOUNTS 198

Choosing an Email Provider.. *198*
Buying Your Own Domain Name *199*
Setting Up Email Accounts in Outlook... *201*
Understanding POP3 vs. IMAP... *201*
Collecting the needed information for setup *202*
Setting up an account using automatic settings *204*
Setting up an account using manual settings... *205*
Modifying Mail Account Settings.. *206*
Changing the Mail Server... *207*
Sending Messages from Different Accounts *209*

CHAPTER 13 211

MERGING MAIL FROM OUTLOOK TO MICROSOFT WORD 211

Making Mailing Label Magic.. *211*
Urging merger... *211*
Making and using a merge template... *214*
Understanding Formal Letter Formalities.. *215*
Merging Contacts from Selected Lists *217*
You'll Still Have to Lick It: Printing Envelopes *217*
Email Merging *218*

CHAPTER 14 219

BIG-TIME COLLABORATION WITH OUTLOOK 219

Collaborating with Outlook's Help... *219*
Organizing a meeting.. *220*
Responding to a meeting request *223*
Checking responses to your meeting request *225*
Taking a vote... *226*
Tallying votes.. *227*
Assigning tasks *228*
Sending a status report *228*
Collaborating with Outlook and Exchange... *229*
Giving the delegate permission *230*
Opening someone else's folder.. *231*
Viewing Two Calendars Side by Side.. *232*

Setting access permissions... 233
Looking at two accounts... 235
Managing Your Out of Office Message 236
Managing Your Address Books 238
Scheduling a Skype Meeting 240
Setting up a Skype meeting 240
Joining a Skype meeting 240

CHAPTER 15 242

OUTLOOK FOR THE IPAD AND ANDROID PHONES 242

Understanding the Mobile Difference... 242
Using Mobile Email 243
Reading email.. 243
Replying to email 243
Composing an email... 244
Archiving, scheduling, and deleting email messages................................ 245
Deleting messages 247
Managing groups of messages... 248
Using Your Mobile Calendar 248
Navigating the mobile calendar 249
Creating a new appointment 249

CHAPTER 16 251

TELECOMMUTING WITH OUTLOOK.COM AND THE OUTLOOK WEB APP
.... 251

Signing In to Outlook.com... 251
Exploring the Outlook.com Interface 252
GETTING CAUGHT UP ON WEB EMAIL BASICS.. 253
Reading messages 254
Sending a message.. 254
Choosing the message's importance.. 255
Flagging messages... 255
Organizing Contacts... 255
Viewing the contacts 256
Adding contacts 256
Using Your Calendar 257
Viewing your calendar 257

Entering an appointment *258*
Moving to an appointment *259*
Exploring Your Options *260*
Automated vacation replies or out of office messages *260*
Creating a signature *261*
Understanding the Outlook Web App *262*
Knowing when it's handy *262*
Signing in and out *263*

CHAPTER 17 264

TEN SHORTCUTS WORTH TAKING 264

USING THE NEW ITEMS TOOL 264
Sending a File to an Email Recipient *265*
Sending a File From a Microsoft Office Application *266*
Turning a Message Into a Meeting *267*
Finding Something *267*
Undoing Your Mistakes *267*
Using the "Go to Date" Dialog Box *268*
Adding Items to List Views *268*
Sending Repeat Messages *268*
Resending a Message *269*

CHAPTER 18 271

TEN ACCESSORIES FOR OUTLOOK 271
Smartphones *271*
A Tablet Computer *271*
E-Learning *272*
Microsoft Office *272*
A Business-Card Scanner *273*
Online Backup *273*
Skype *273*
Microsoft SharePoint *274*
Microsoft Exchange *274*
OneDrive *275*

CHAPTER 19 276

TEN THINGS YOU CAN'T DO WITH OUTLOOK 276

Create a Unified Inbox	276
Adding a Phone Number to Your Calendar	277
Open a Message From the Reading Pane	277
Performing Two-sided Printing	277
Searching and Replacing Area Codes	278
Printing a List of Meeting Attendees	278
Enlarging the Type in the Calendar Location Box	278
Creating Contact Records for All Email Recipients	279
Tracking Meeting Time Zones	279
Easily Backup Outlook Data	280

CHAPTER 20 281

TEN THINGS YOU CAN DO AFTER YOU'RE COMFORTABLE 281

Customizing the Quick Access Toolbar	281
Wising Up Your Messages with Smart Art	282
Including Impact Charts	283
Opening a number of calendars	284
Superimpose Calendars	285
Selecting Dates as a Group	285
Pin a Contact Card	286
CONCLUSION	286

INDEX 288

INTRODUCTION

Microsoft Outlook is a personal resource management system software created by Microsoft and is also available as part of the Microsoft suite. Though it is primarily an email client, it also has other functions which include calendaring, managing tasks, managing contacts, note-taking, web browsing, and journal jogging, amongst others.

While Outlook can be used by individuals as a stand-alone application, organizations make use of it as a multi-user software (through the use of Microsoft Exchange Server and also SharePoint) for the use of shared functions such as mailboxes, folders, data gathering, and the scheduling of various appointments.

Microsoft has designed applications for use on most mobile platforms, which include Apple iOS and Android. Furthermore, all data in Outlook Mobile can be synced from Windows Phone devices. With the use of Microsoft Visual Studio, developers now know how to create their unique custom software that can be used with Outlook and other Office packages.

Just like that of the desktop version, Outlook mobile provides an aggregation of attachments and files that are saved on cloud storage platforms; a "focused inbox" that highlights messages from contacts that are used frequently; the addition of calendar events, files, and the inclusion of locations to messages without the need to switch apps. The application also provides support for various emailing platforms and services like Outlook.com, Microsoft Exchange, and Google Workspace, formerly known as the G Suite, amongst others.

Outlook Mobile was created to bring together functionality that was normally supposed to be found in different applications on mobile devices that are close to the personal information managers on PCs. It is created around four major hubs, which include mail, calendar, files, and people. The people hub regularly enlists contacts and aggregates communication that is used often with them, and the files hub also has a way of aggregating messages and also allows you to integrate with other storage devices online like Dropbox, Google Drive, and OneDrive.

Outlook provides support for various email services and platforms, which include Exchange and iCloud. Google Workspace, Outlook.com, and Yahoo Mail. The application also supports the use of different email accounts at once. Just like the desktop version of Outlook, Outlook Mobile enables users to see appointment details and also reply to exchange meeting invites and schedule meetings. It also adds the three-day view option and lovely calendar options from Sunrise.

As of March 2020, Microsoft announced the launch of a series of new products to appeal to business customers of its Team platform, in addition to the products that were introduced the month before. The chat and collaborative modules now have more efficient and integrated waypoints specifically created to make group work for organizations simple and to also give encouragement to such an organization to use the Microsoft platform to become the preferred company chat platform.

With the very first version of Outlook being Outlook 97 version 8.0, released on the 16th of January, 1997, Microsoft has now released a better and more packed version. Outlook 2019, version 16 was released on the 24th of September, 2018, and is also included in the 2019 Office Suite and also the online version, i.e., Office 365.

Some of the features of Outlook 2019 include a focused inbox, the inclusion of multiple time zones, the option of listening to emails rather than just reading them, a much easier and faster way of sorting email, an automatic download of attachments to the cloud, and also the True Dark Mode that helps to reduce the brightness of the screen and also increases the life span of the battery.

CHAPTER 1

OUTLOOK FEATURES YOU NEED TO KNOW

Explaining Why So Many People Use Outlook

Most people prefer to make use of Outlook rather than Gmail accounts.

Outlined below are some of the reasons:

Its compatibility with email, contacts, and calendars. The main mode of communication, especially in business, today remains email. Most users opt for the option that Outlook has just one place for effective communication at work for things to get done effectively. It doesn't matter if it is to have meetings organized, the need to gather more information about a contact, having to put a call through a conference call, or jump into an online meeting, Outlook seems to be the perfect hub. Users say Outlook helps them get through their daily tasks without having to think too much. Each Morning Outlook has been designed in such a way as to wake them each morning by reminding them of their activities that have been scheduled for the day.

Offline access to email messages

Outlook provides users the option to access their emails when they are not connected to the internet. This means users can catch up with work-related mail even when they are on a plane and have the airplane mode on their phones turned on. Most of them also work on Outlook throughout their journey, since they can read and respond to email just like they would if there were an internet connection. Once the internet connection is established, the messages will be sent automatically.

In total contrast, Gmail only gives access to email messages from the previous months once there is no internet connection, which can only be accessed in an offline mode on Chrome and Safari browsers. Outlook does not have such restrictions.

A customized mode of organizing email

Not everyone likes to work alphabetically sorting through their folders. Some like to make use of the search box to find their email, while others enjoy the use of specific bins to search for their mail. This makes the use of Outlook more rampant. In comparison to Outlook, users have fewer options for organizing their emails on other platforms. They are limited to the use of just labels to organize their email.

Grouping email items for better organization

With the use of Outlook, users can attach groups to different items like calendars, appointments, etc. An item can be used to attach to different groups to have them classified in more than just one way. At the slightest glance, users can see how their time is spent across various areas by just looking at the color-coding of the events on the calendar. Those who make use of groupings and color-coding to keep their work organized won't be able to imagine how they would cope without them. Google has rendered color-coding useless due to its inability to differentiate items in their different boxes through the use of colors.

Rules to reduce the clutter of email

With the use of Outlook and the consistent push to upgrade the app, Microsoft has found a way to better manage the clutter in the box even as research is ongoing to make progress in that regard every day. Gmail is equipped to filter, but the actions that should be taken after the filtering of the emails are quite limited. Setting up very important rules to flag important emails based on the sender of the message is much easier with the use of Outlook.

Access to rich contact information

The experience shared when being able to locate a person's office with the use of their contact card is simply amazing. The contact card in Outlook provides a lot of rich information about a person. The picture in the contact card also helps users link people's faces with their names. "Presence" information displays the status of the user if they are either busy, online, or offline. Users can also start a chat, book an appointment, have a quick chat over the phone, or start an online conference. Unlike Google mail and other platforms, the contact card in Outlook has a person's job title, department, and also their location information.

Scheduling meetings

With the use of Outlook, users can schedule and reschedule resources such as meeting rooms, projectors, etc., just by including them as a resource in the meeting. The resource will then perform like any other attendee and also includes the ability to respond automatically to the meeting invite and the ability to see busy schedules and those that are free. Reports state that attempting to perform this function on other platforms, especially Google Mail, can be very frustrating as it is a cumbersome multi-step process that involves primary and secondary calendars.

The ability to ignore conversations

Not all conversations are worth responding to; some are meant to simply be ignored. Most such conversations are possible outcomes of a person's oversight or who has the last say attitude. Outlook has a very unique way of ignoring such conversations. With a simple click, all present and new emails in that conversation will be moved to the deleted items folder. This will also help to remove clutter from the inbox and also help focus on more important tasks.

Users also like the cleanup option. This way, only the latest email thread with all comments will be kept. The rest of the emails will then be moved to the deleted items folder. All unique conversations will still be kept in one place, but with Gmail, users will only have the option to mute conversations. This ability is not discovered easily, and it will not work if the recipient gets re-added to the line of the email.

Sharing and delegating calendars

Users who are administrative assistants have revealed how tedious it is to have to work with Google Calendar. They believe that with the use of Google calendar, there is no other option apart from sharing all the details on the calendar or just the free/busy schedule. It cannot share the free/busy with the subject of the events because it does not have the level of control as to the details that should and shouldn't be shared.

When they switched over to Outlook from Gmail, they had much better control over the management of calendars. For example, they could decide if they need to share a person's free or busy status as well as the subject of the meeting, attendees, the location, etc. Once the calendar has been assigned, the administrative assistants can also manage the assigned calendars with their own calendars in a very simple and unique way, which will also reduce the confusion of adjusting the wrong calendar.

The very important thing Outlook offers is the ability for it to be used in a way that brings about more productivity in the job, be it as an administrative assistant, helping the team lead, or even for personal use. The availability of various choices and flexibility is what is missed the most with Outlook.

The Easiest Way to Do Anything in Outlook

Outlook manages email, calendar, contacts, and other tasks all in just one hub. Hence, its steady growth since 2017 doesn't come as a surprise. Here are some ways to carry out major tasks in Outlook easily. Allow Outlook to communicate with you.

When we say Outlook talking, it's not really as you may presume, it's simply having to engage Microsoft's Cortana productivity assistant. Once Cortana has been set up in Outlook, there is an option to listen to new emails as opposed to reading them. By speaking only, messages can be listened to, flagged, deleted, and also replied to. Cortana doesn't only help to read emails; he or she can also help to keep things organized. The AI will feed you in on the changes to events and also pick out schedules that clash with others on the calendar.

Using a focus box

Cluttered inboxes can be an uphill task to scroll through. Scan through messages easily with the use of the focused inbox. There is an option to make two identical inboxes, one focused and the other unfocused. You can then toggle between the two with the use of a simple button slide at the top of the inbox.

Outlook can help get mail sorted, moving important messages to "focused" and transferring junk mail to "others". There is always an option to reclassify messages by moving them from one section of the inbox to another. The "Always move to focus" option can also be selected or otherwise if there is a need for communication from that particular sender to appear at a particular place. The interesting thing about the focused inbox is that the more it is used, the smarter it gets, i.e., the ability to depict junk from real messages. It is sensitive to how emails are sorted with the aim of better classifying incoming messages and helping to focus only on what matters.

Share Calendars

Oftentimes, a lot of time is wasted in meetings. While that is being worked on with various organizations, Outlook removes the inefficiency of trying to fix another meeting again.

With the use of shared calendars in Outlook, get to the calendar settings and choose the people you would love to share it with, such as friends, family, or colleagues at work. You can use the color-code option for the different people that you share with and also control their permissions to let them either share, view, edit, or manage the calendar. Details that will be shared can also be chosen between all, only title and locations, or only when I am busy.

Make use of the scheduling assistant

When sharing calendars, there is an option to make use of the schedule assistant instead of having to always send emails to come up with a time to get together. Make an event on the calendar, then add the people that should be invited. The schedule assistant time picker can then be used to drag and drop to a time on the calendar that turns green. This means everyone is available for the meeting.

Get people's attention by mentioning them

When working alongside someone or in a team, saying "Hey Jane", i.e., mentioning the person's specific name, will draw the person's attention. The same can be done with the use of Outlook's @ mentions. When you type "@ Jane" in an email, the person will see that they have been called into a conversion. Furthermore, when people @ mention you, the inbox will show the important sentences that surround the @ mention in the message excerpt. With this, you will know what you need to do at a glance

Customizing the swipe options

In a dating app, for instance, it is expected that you swipe either left or right to pick a potential match. You can be decisive in an Outlook inbox as well. Open Outlook settings and choose from the selections below; delete, mark as read, mark as unread, flag, or archive.

Using Email: Basic Delivery Techniques

If you are new to Microsoft Outlook, follow the instructions listed for the "initial setup of an email account."

Initial Setup of an Email Account

- When Microsoft Outlook 2019 is opened for the first time, the select profile window will be displayed. Confirm the profile when done by selecting the **OK button.**

- The welcome to Outlook 2019 will then be displayed. Click **on the Next button.**

- Insert **the email address.**

- Click **on the advanced options button.**

- Select **I'd like to set up my account manually.**

- Click **on the connect button.** Then choose the account type window that will open.

- If you prefer to check your email with the use of IMAP (recommended), choose **the IMAP account type**. If there is a need to check your email using POP3, choose the POP account type.

Reading email

To read email messages with the use of Outlook, simply follow the steps below.

- Click **the Inbox.** This will display a list of messages.

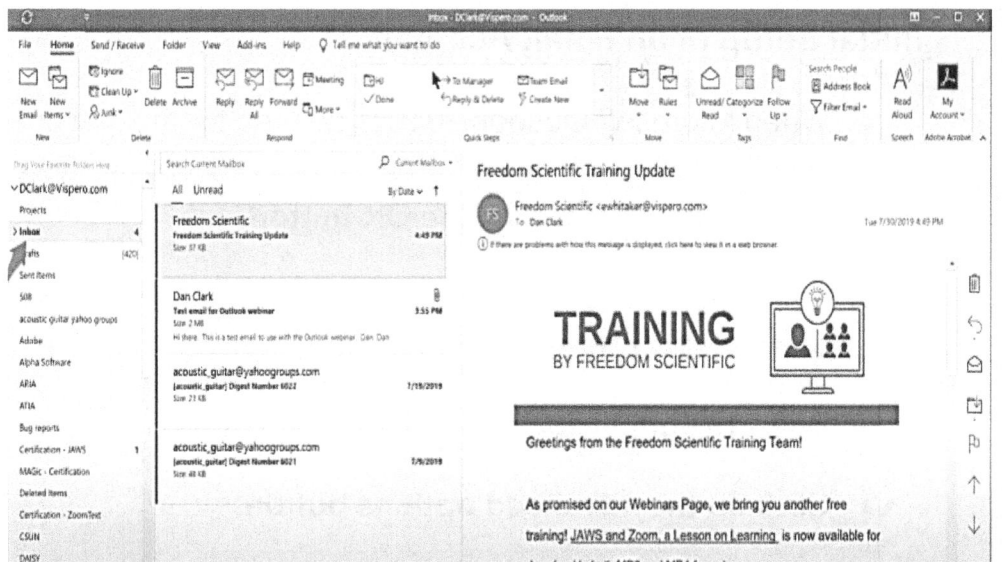

- Click **on the messages you want to read.** The message text will then be displayed in the reading pane on the right side or lower part of the screen. As each of the messages is clicked, the contents of the messages will then show up in the reading pane.

Note: There is also an option to make use of the arrow keys to move from one email message to the next.

Click **on the icon that appears to be like a gear (on the far right side of the ribbon) to make adjustments to the mail settings.**

The reading pane can also be opened on the right or in the lower part of the screen, and it can also be completely closed. If the reading pane is closed, there will be a need to **double-click any message to view it in another window**.

Answering email

- In the message list, select **the message that should be replied to.**

- Right click **on the message** > Choose **the reply or reply all option**.

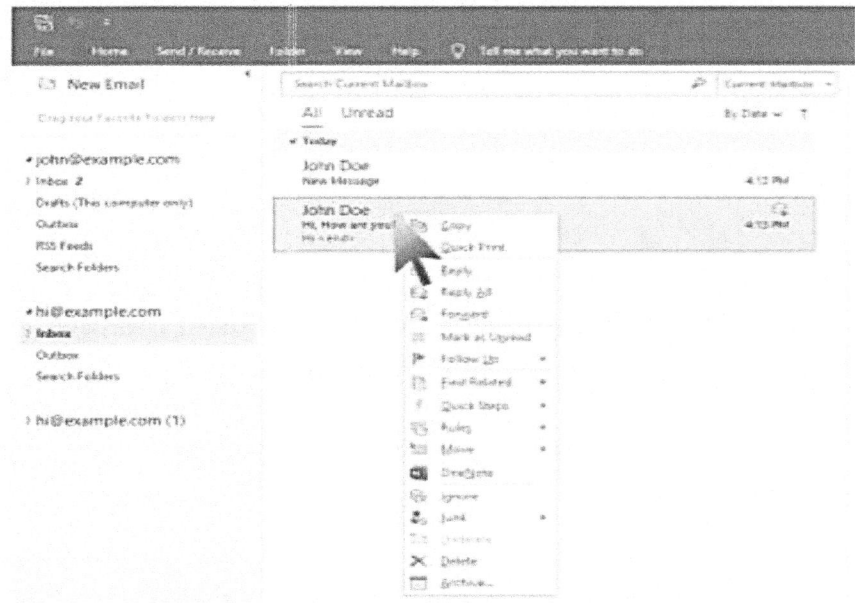

- Type the response and then click on **the "send" button**.

Creating new email messages

- Navigate **to the top of the page and choose the new email option**.

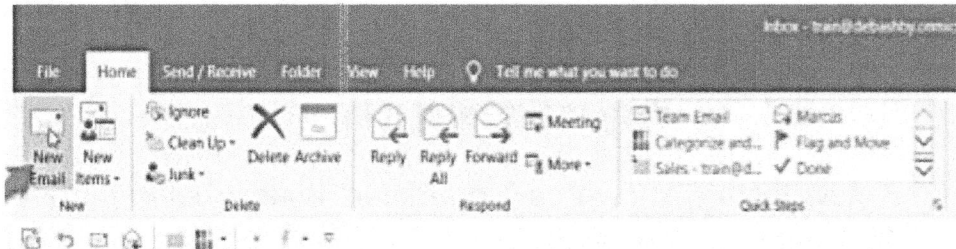

- On the To line, insert **the name or email address of the person whom the message is meant for**.

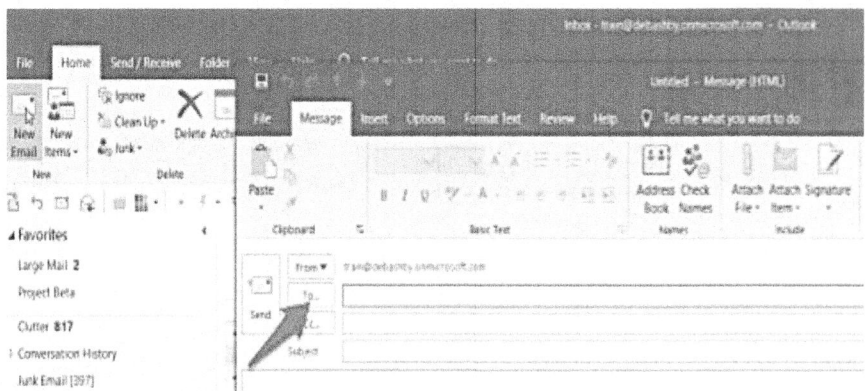

- In the Add, a subject line, insert **a brief description of what the message should be about.**

- To have a file attached to the message, click on **the attach button.**

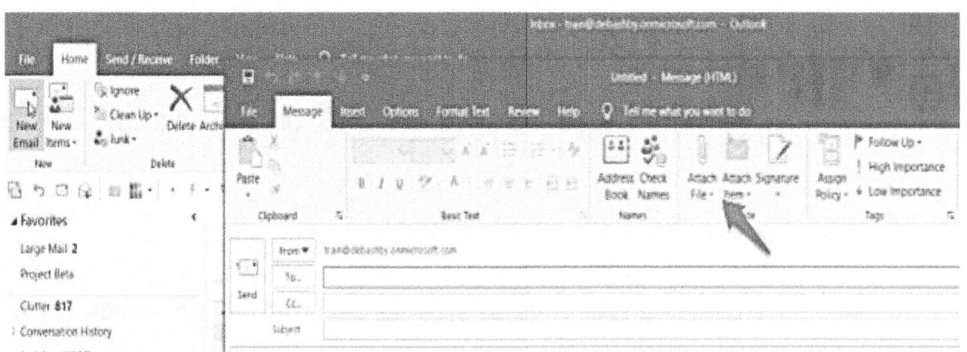

- Type the message and then click **on the "send" button.**

Schedule sending mail; send it later.

A new feature known as "send later" is now being introduced to Outlook. This feature will allow users to be able to defer sending an email and then choose a particular date and time when the email should be sent. To do this, simply follow the steps below.

- Compose the email message.

- Click **on send and send later.**

- Choose **the preferred date and time when the message should be sent.**

- Finally, click **on the send button.**

Note: The message will always remain in the drafts or sent items folder (based on the device) until it is time for it to be sent. There is also an option to either edit or delete the message at any time until it is meant to be sent. After making adjustments to the message, select the send and send later option. Note that it is not compulsory to have access to the internet when the message is scheduled to be sent.

Forwarding an email message

"Forwarding a message" simply means sending an already existing message without making any adjustments to it.

To forward a message, simply follow the steps below.

- Locate the message list and select the message that should be forwarded.

- Navigate **to the top right-hand corner of the message pane** > choose **the select button or select and then select forward**.

- When the message that should be forwarded is already in the message box, select **the send button**.

It is worthwhile to note that only one message can be forwarded at a time. When a message is forwarded, the original message will remain in the mailbox, and a copy will be sent to the new recipient.

Sending a File

Most of the daily work is likely done in programs other than Outlook. Documents might be made in Microsoft Word or spreadsheets created in Excel. When there is a need to send a file by email, Outlook becomes involved, though there are times it works in the background. A file can be shared by sending a link to a file that has been saved on OneDrive. If the file cannot be found on OneDrive, there will be a prompt to have a copy saved on it before the file can be shared.

To send a file as a link, follow these steps:

- Open **the document that should be sent in Microsoft Word**.

- Once the document has been opened on the screen, click **on the share option in the upper right corner of the Word window**.

- Once the share dialog box is displayed, select **the One Drive option**.

The share dialog box will be displayed if the file has not been saved on OneDrive. Note that the file has to be saved on OneDrive before the link can be shared (if there is no need to save the file on OneDrive, follow the next steps below to share the file).

- Locate **the share task pane** and then insert **the email address of the person that the file is intended to be sent to.** To insert more than one address, separate the addresses with semicolons.

- If there is no need for the recipient to have control over editing the file, click **on the "can edit" drop-down menu and select the "can view" option**. These settings will determine if the recipient will be made to make adjustments to the files.

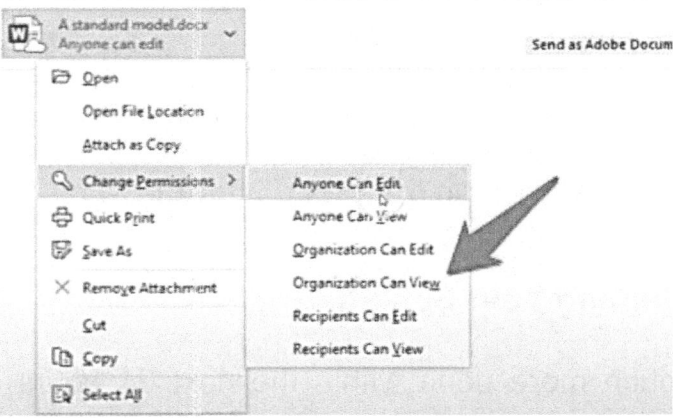

- Fill in the message box with a message for the recipient. The message will then be displayed as the email message body.

- Finally, click **on the share option.**

To send a file as an attachment, follow the steps below.

- **Open the document that should be sent in Microsoft Word**.

- Once **the document opens on the screen**, click **on the "Share" button in the upper right** corner of the Microsoft Word window. This button offers a very quick way to share. There is also an option to use the file share option.

- If the share dialog box is displayed, click **on Word Document,** or rather, if the share task pane displays, click **on the send as attachment option** and then click **on Send a copy.** Notwithstanding the method used, the new message form will be opened with the document displayed in the attached line. If you prefer to type a message in the body of the screen, you can go ahead, but it is not compulsory.

- Insert **the email address of the person the message is intended for**. To insert more than one address, separate them with a semicolon.

- You can tweak the subject line if need be.

- Finally, click **on the "send" button.**

Maintaining Your Schedule

Get much more done within the next 24 hours if the Microsoft Outlook 2019 calendar is kept current. Appointments can be entered and managed from right within Outlook.

Opening an appointment in Outlook

If at any point in time you have had to use the old method of planning with the use of paper, the Outlook calendar will be very familiar to you.

- Select **the calendar button in the navigation bar**.
- Click **on the Day button on the Home tab and a grid in the middle of the screen lines that shows each segment of the day will be displayed**. The length of these segments can also be tweaked from as little as 5 minutes to as much as 60 minutes.

To enter an appointment at a certain time, follow the steps below:

- If need be, click **on the calendar located in the navigation bar to change to the calendar module if needed**.
- Enter a name for the appointment.
- Click **on the next line at the very time the appointment is supposed to begin**.

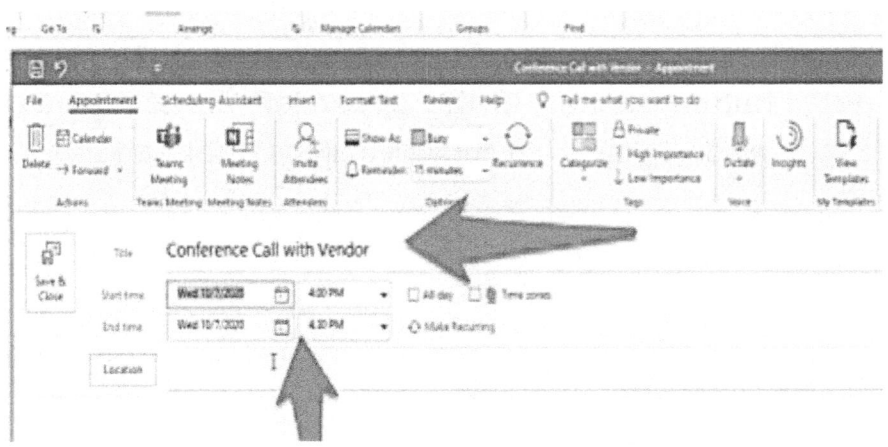

- Finally, **click on the enter button**.

Time management has a lot to do with more than just inserting appointments. In any case, if you are busy, there might be a need to manage the time by slicing and dicing the list of appointments to see when you are free to add additional appointments.

If there is a need to have a more broad collection of calendar views, select the view tab located on the ribbon and then make a choice from the views listed under the change view button.

Adding a contact

Typically, Microsoft Outlook refers to the information stored about people and organizations as "contact information." It also stores this information in a folder known as Contacts. To gain access to the contact folder, select the contacts icon (which has an image of two people) located in the lower-left corner of the Outlook window. The contact folder then shows each of the contacts that have been entered into Outlook.

To store a person's contact information, follow the following steps:

- Locate **the contacts window**, select **the "New contact" button located in the upper left corner**. A new contact window that is untitled will then be displayed.

- Fill in the information that needs to be saved for the person or organization. You can fill it in as much or as little as you want.

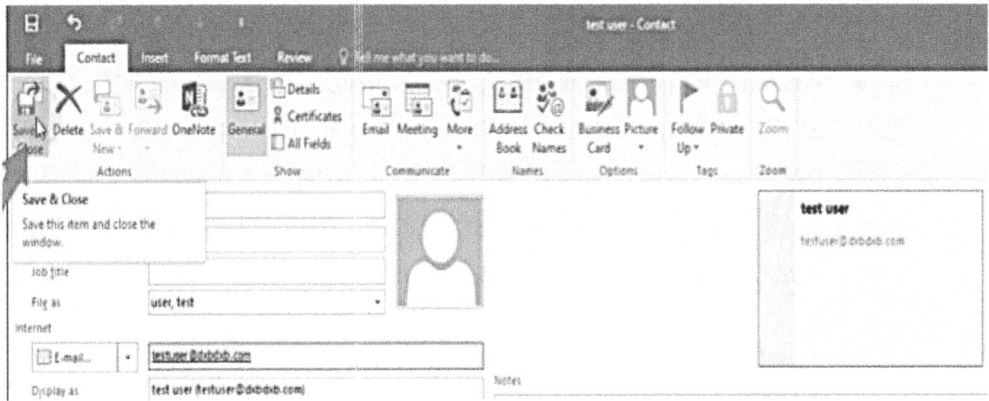

- Finally, **click on the save and close button located on the ribbon**. The contact will then be added to your contact list.

Here are some tidbits that should be considered when entering contact information:

- Anything that is typed in the Full Name Field will immediately replace the word "Untitled" in the dialog box title bar.

- In the File As field, the mode in which the entry is alphabetized is defined. The default is by the last name, and it will reverse whatever name that is entered in the full name field. For example, if the name entered is Mark Joe in the full name field, it will appear as Joe, Mark. For people's names, this can be the best way to go about it, but for a company's name like ACME Corporation, it might probably not be the best for it to be alphabetized as Corporation, ACME. To have that fixed, open the File As drop-down list and select ACME Corporation.

- Multiple email addresses can be saved for one person. Notice that email is not just a field label, it is also a drop-down list. Open the list and select Email 2, Email 3, and so on for the additional addresses.

- All phone number fields also have drop-down lists that are in association with their labels. Up to four phone numbers can be saved for one person, and a label for each of the numbers can be carried. For example, the label "mobile" can be assigned to one of the phone numbers.

- There can be up to three addresses for one person: business, home, and other. You can toggle between these addresses with the drop-down list in the addresses section.

- When an address is entered but wasn't entered in the proper mailing format (address, city, state, and zip code), a dialog box will pop up so that that information can be filed in. This is to protect you, as it will ensure that every address entered is usable.

- Make use of the Notes pane to store any other additional information about the person that doesn't correspond with any of the fields stored.

- The default fields that are displayed are known as "general fields." There are also more fields available. Navigate **to the contact tab**, move to the show group, and select **details to see the other fields**.

- To customize the appearance of the contacts, select **from sets of fields rather than the defaults.**

Entering a Task

It is not enough to know what to do; there is a need to always know what to do next till the task is completed. When you are working on a lot of demands, there is a need for a tool that helps in showing what should be done next at a simple glance so that the work can keep moving without an abrupt stop.

Microsoft Outlook has a lot of task management tools that can be of use in the organization of lengthy to-do lists in order to obtain maximum performance. The tools include the tasks module. The to-do lists and the to-do bar below are a quick way to get started.

To enter a new task, simply follow the steps below:

- Locate the navigation bar and select **Tasks to change to the Tasks module if there is a need for it.**

- On the Home tab of the Ribbon in the Current View group,

Select Simple List to ensure the task list is in the Simple List view. New tasks can be created from just about any view, but the wording of the step that follows is a little different based on the view that is being used, so the choice of views is just to avoid any form of confusion when getting started with Outlook.

- Select **"Click here to include a new task box"** and then type in the name of the task. In some of the views, the wording used is "Type a New Task," and in other views, the box for adding a new task with this method is not present at all. This is why it is best to start in the Simple List view to completely avoid any form of confusion.

- When all has been completed, tap the enter key and the new task will be moved down to the task list with the other tasks.

With the use of Outlook, you can manage just about anything perfectly. From a simple shopping list to a complex business project.

Taking Notes

Almost everyone makes use of sticky notes to set reminders for themselves, from bits of information to website passwords or some memorable quotes. Outlook also has notes, which are the electronic equivalent of sticky notes. Anything can be stored on a note, but they are best used for the storage of little pieces of information like confirmation codes, pins, or membership ID numbers. A note can be left open as long as Outlook is also open. This way, you will always be reminded each time it is seen or have the note closed so that it won't be in your way.

To make a note, simply follow the steps below:

- Show the notes portion of Outlook. To get this done,

Click on **the More icon in the bottom left corner of the window**, and in the menu that is displayed, **click Notes**.

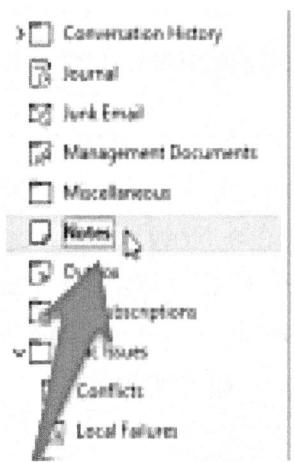

- Select **Home, then click on "New Note"** or use **the keyboard shortcut and press Ctrl + N.** A new blank note will then be displayed. Type in whatever you want on this new blank note. Note that the first few words of the first line will be displayed in the form of an icon title. Try as much as possible to be descriptive there. But if you are trying to be secretive about the information, like a password, there might be a need for some misleading words in the first line. You can decide to keep passwords in a note that is titled "Family Birthdays." With this, if anyone wants to snoop or steal passwords, the person wouldn't care about "Family Birthdays" and would simply pass that by.

- Close the note by simply clicking **on the X button located in the upper right corner**, and the note will be saved automatically.

Below are some useful Outlook note tidbits.

- To open a note again, simply place the mouse arrow on the note and double-click on it. The note will then remain open until it is closed again or Outlook is exited.

- To move a note, drag it around with the use of its title bar (the colored bar at the very top of the note), placing it wherever you like on-screen, even beyond the boundaries of the Outlook window. The note will remain there until Outlook is closed.

- To make adjustments to a note, **open the note by double-clicking** and then make the necessary changes to it.

- To change the size of the note, click **on the note and drag its bottom right corner.**

- **To have a note deleted, click on the note and follow these steps:**

    - Select **Home,** then **Delete.**

    - Press the **delete key** on the keyboard or **right-click** on the **note.**

    - Select the **Delete option** from the menu that is displayed.

To restore a note that has been deleted, open the Mail portion of Outlook, show the contents of the Deleted Items folder, find the note, and then move it to the Notes icon that can be found in the bottom left corner of the window.

There is also an option to;

- Right-click **on the note.**

- Select the **Move to Folder option**, which then indicates the very part that it should be moved to.

Categorizing Outlook notes

Given that a note is an incredibly versatile item, creating categories for it might be very useful. This way, one will be able to differentiate one type of note from the other. By assigning a color to a note, the type of information the note should contain can be specified. For example, you can decide to make financial notes green in color and make family notes blue.

Follow the steps below to apply a color to a category note.

- Right-click **on the note and select the option to categorize**. A menu of color choices will then be displayed.

- Click on **the preferred color**.

If this category has been used once, that is all at this point. The notes icon and background will change to the color chosen. However, the first time a certain color is used, the Rename Category dialog box will be opened. This way, a name can be assigned. Outlook does not assign any special meaning to color; it is best done based on personal preference. If there is a prompt, change the name in the Name box and then click on the **OK button**.

Keep in mind that if the default email account is of the IMAP type, the Categories option won't be displayed. Should this option not be displayed, do not panic. Just check the email account.

If there is a need to rename a category, simply follow the steps below:

- Click **Home**, then Categories, and then All Categories. The color categories in the dialog box will then be open.

- Click on **the preferred category** and click **on the rename button**. The name then becomes editable.

- Finally, type in the new name and press **the Enter key.**

You can also add and delete categories and alter the color associated with a category. For instance, this might be useful if you wanted to have the color used to represent a particular category changed, but you don't want to lose the category information already attached to existing notes. Note that it is possible to have up to 25 categories.

A note can have different categories assigned to it. Each category is an on or off switch for each note. A note icon will show only the color of the category that was last assigned to it, but it will still keep other categories as well.

To remove a category from a note;

- Click on the **note** and select **"home."**

- **Categorize,** and then click on the specific category to switch it off for that particular note.

Categories are also shared by the calendar and tasks features in Outlook. As categories are being created, it is necessary to keep in mind how you might prefer to categorize appointments and events also.

CHAPTER 2

GETTING MORE DONE WITH LESS EFFORT

In this chapter, we will delve more deeply into how Outlook works, its components, and how much can be achieved without spending a lot of time trying to figure out how things work. Carefully go through the points outlined below to gain more knowledge.

Outlook and Other Programs

Lots of users prefer to use Outlook as their email client and personal information manager. Over the years, Outlook, as part of the Microsoft Office Suite, has proven to be a standard solution (in conjunction with the Microsoft Exchange Server) for both public and private organizations.

Even though without a doubt, Outlook is the option to beat, many freelancers and small companies cannot afford solutions intended for larger businesses, but there are lots of email management programs aside from Outlook that can be used for free. Some of which are

Postbox

This program was created by one-time Mozilla employees and hence was based on Thunderbird. About ten years later, the software has developed into an autonomous and extremely effective mail client. The design of its interface is like that of other solutions, and it is also easy to use. Users who want a unique look can adjust themes or design their templates.

For a more efficient operation, Postbox makes use of different shortcuts. Users can access the Quick Bar via hotkey so that messages can be moved or categorized quickly. In addition, when creating an email, a signature can be entered with the use of the Quick Bar without having to use the mouse.

There are lots of benefits when writing emails in the postbox. The software has various templates and text blocks that can be used to write cover letters and replies in a placeholder that can be added and created where the name of the receiver is always added automatically.

Thunderbird

For both private users and those in companies, Thunderbird is one of the most preferred options as an alternative to Outlook. The open-source solution is also available for free. The free version of the program is rather streamlined and offers only the most basic functions. One major advantage is the addition of various add-ons. This means that there is room for expansion for the email program. However, the add-ons and extensions are made to suit their respective versions. If there is a need to update your version of Thunderbird, the add-ons must be updated as well.

Spike

Spike was released in the year 2013 and it combines certain functions of classic email programs with those that are used in modern messenger apps. Immediately a private mailbox is linked to the application, elements like subjects or signatures are no longer necessary, while the basic mail client functions, which include the central inbox or contact management, will be integrated into the modern messenger environment. It is also not coincidental that the creator of Spike described it as a conversational email application. Note that both audio and video calls can also be made via the software.

The spike depends on modern standards in terms of security. With just a single click, communications that also include attached files can be encrypted. This way, you can be sure your messages are fully protected against unwanted access. Spike is free for private users; however, monthly fees are charged when business email accounts are added.

Mailbird

Mailbird is an Outlook alternative that is only free in the test version. This email solution allows the unification of messages and contacts from different accounts into just one box. With different free themes, the interface can be designed as it best suits you.

Mailbird offers different interfaces to various applications and also enhances the mailbox with helpful features for better interaction and teamwork. For instance, Twitter, Whatsapp, Calendar, and Dropbox can be integrated into the mail to change it to a multi-functional program.

Outlook's Main Screen

Using the Folder pane

The folder pane shows all the folders in Outlook. If this pane is minimized, other folders will not be displayed and you will not be able to gain access to them. There are two different ways this folder can be viewed.

The first is by;

- Clicking **on the left side of the screen**. This will help in expanding the folder pane, making other folders visible.

- The second option is to click **on view**, then the folder pane, click **on normal so as to see things in a clearer way**.

The folder pane in Outlook is said to be the main navigation tool between mailboxes, folders, and different modules like mail, calendar, and contacts. Note that the folder pane has a couple of different options and tips that can help make the pane fit more into your kind of style and help you work effectively and efficiently.

You can choose to enable or even disable the folder pane by Pressing **the ALT + F1 buttons**.

To change from one module to the other, make use of the icons enlisted in the lower area of the Folder pane. If you also prefer to see the names of the modules alone instead, disable the Compact Navigation through the Folder Pane Options dialog box.

Note that with the use of the Folder Pane, you can configure the way modules are shown and in the very order they are shown; they can also show module icons or names for easy navigation; add shortcuts to modules; and lots more.

To get the best out of this folder, you should spend some time clicking on **various options**, including the ones explained above.

The Information Viewer: Outlook's hotspot

The information viewer is the very place where most of the action in Outlook takes place. If we can assume the folder pane as being the channel sector on a TV, the information viewer will be more like the TV screen.

The information viewer is the very place where emails are read, contacts are searched for or added, and contact names are also displayed. If you also wish to do a whole lot of other fancy things like sorting contacts, tasks, and so on, the information viewer is the perfect place to get all of that and more done.

Based on the fact that lots of information, more than what can be seen at a glance, can be stored in Outlook, the information viewer helps to show a preview of the information available. This way, you are up to date with all you need to know. The calendar, for example, can store dates as far back as the 16's and as far ahead as you can imagine. The smallest calendar review that can be displayed is a day, and the largest calendar view is a month.

The information viewer also helps to arrange what it displays into smaller units known as "views." There is an option to create your own views and also save them, but you can also decide to use the view that comes with Outlook.

Move through the different previews of the information displayed by Outlook by clicking on various parts of the information viewer. Some people love to say they are browsing the information viewer when moving around it; it seems more like just scanning through the pages of a notebook.

You can also browse through the calendar data in the information viewer to keep you abreast of things to come.

To do that, simply follow the steps below:

- Click **on the calendar in the navigation bar** or make use of the keyboard shortcut and press the Ctrl + 2 buttons.

- Next, click **on the workweek button located** on the Home tab of the ribbon. The workweek view of the calendar will then be displayed. Note that a workweek means 5 days if the regular calendar week shows 7 days.

To further spice things up, you can decide to change the appearance of the information viewer in several ways. For example, there might be a need to see the schedule for just a day or just the items that have been fixed for a particular category. Views can ensure that you get a glance at the very preview of information needed.

While checking out the calendar, you can also decide to check the To-Do bar located on the right side of the screen. The To-Do bar shows the appointments you have and also reminds you of things you need to do. To turn on this feature,

- Click on **the View tab located on the ribbon** > click on **the To-Do Bar** > click **the calendar button**.

In Outlook, every module (mail, calendar, people, tasks, etc.) has its own version of the Ribbon, arranged specifically to meet the needs of the module. Most of all the buttons are visibly labeled with the very actions they are used for, such as replies, business cards, new appointments, and lots more.

A little button known as "properties" can be found in the lower-right corner of some groups.

- Click on **it if you want more information displayed than what is shown on the ribbon**. Properties are also known as "dialog boxes" as they open some sort of dialog box launcher related to the group when it is clicked.

The Ribbon Ties

Viewing Screen Tips

Each button located on the ribbon shows a little popup known as a "ScreenTip" when the mouse is placed over it. The ScreenTip informs you about the name of the button and also tells you things that will happen if you click on the button.

Some buttons have a small arrow that points downwards or to the right side of the button.

Click on **the arrow to have a menu or list open**. A very popular example, pertinent to almost all the modules in Outlook on the Home tab, is a button known as "Move." When you click on the Move button, it opens a menu and shows all the various places an Outlook item can be sent to.

Using the New Items Button

Each module in Outlook has a "New Items" button that enables the creation of an item in any module. For instance, if you are checking the name and address of a customer whose name was also mentioned in a very interesting article in one of the daily newspapers, you will want to remember to refer to it at any point in time. You can do this by creating a new item from the new contact option, selecting the particular date, and then saving it with the name of the customer or something unique that can always make you remember the incident in the daily diary.

Finding Things in a Flash with Instant Search

With the use of instant flash, you can find out through anything you want to do in Outlook, simply

Insert the first few words or alphabets and Outlook will bring up suggestions for you.

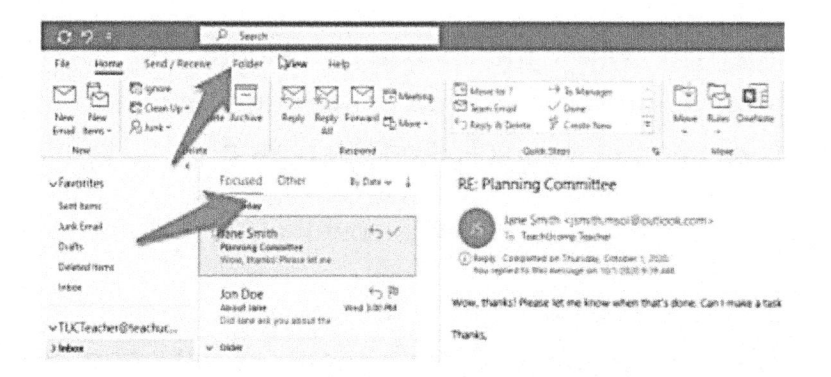

Taking Peeks

One very unique feature in Outlook is a tiny pop-up window known as a "peek," which is displayed when you place your mouse over the modules such as People, Calendar, or Tasks in the navigation bar. This little but unique feature offers great help when giving a reply to an email about an event that needs to be scheduled. Feel free to take a quick peek at your calendar while you continue to work on that particular email. If a broader view with more information is needed, there is an option to make the peek window larger by clicking the button at the top right corner of the peek screen or by double-clicking on the calendar, people, or tasks in the navigation bar.

Getting Help in Outlook

The help feature in the Office applications, which includes Outlook, goes beyond just rendering help as it tries to get things done for you. Does that sound awkward? It isn't, it is just amazing and very helpful.

When working in the help feature, a lightbulb icon and a textbox are located at the top of the screen with the inscription, "Tell me what you want to do." Once that box is clicked, type in what you might need help with and it will display a list of things that starts with a list of things that can be done. For example, if you enter the word "delete," the help feature will bring up a link to the Delete and Delete All commands and also the folder with deleted items. When one of the commands is selected, it will delete the very Outlook item that has been chosen. When you click on "Deleted Items," it will take you straight to the deleted items folder.

Note that it is important that you request only the things that can be done in Outlook. If you type something like "what can I eat?", the choices Outlook will offer you might disappoint you. But if you are trying to do something that involves email, appointments, or tasks, Outlook should provide you with the very important links you need to get things done quickly.

Scroll beneath the list of links to view other choices that might be displayed by Outlook. Once you point at the "Get help" option, it will open a submenu of various help topics that are in some way related to what you have asked. You would have to click on that yourself, as there is no option to help you do that.

The final option in the help menu is called "Smart Lookup," which helps to open the Smart Lookup task pane and makes use of Microsoft Bing, which is the search engine for Microsoft, to search for the phrase that has been entered. When using smart lookup, there may be a need to activate the intelligent service. For example, if you type "marry a millionaire" and click on the smart lookup link, a list of marriageable millionaires will be displayed, and if not, at least At the very least, you will get the definition of the word or phrase that has been typed and probably a link to Wikipedia also.

CHAPTER 3

ON THE FAST TRACK: DRAG TILL YOU DROP

You don't always have to type. In fact, having to type will soon fade away with various inventions in technology. In this dispensation, we seem too stuck with the keyboard. By making use of the mouse, trackball, or touchpad, you can touch and drag an item rather than having to type all the time.

Most people understand that a tool such as Outlook can improve their productivity dramatically, but most of them ignore the productivity of some of its tools, which include tasks and calendars and the ability to sync all your information with ease. Some of these tools can be very powerful weapons in the battle to make the most out of your time.

Dragging

If there is a need to work quickly and easily in Outlook, there is a simple trick called "drag and drop" that offers the opportunity to get things done accurately. This feature is very easy to use, but most people do not take advantage of it. Dragging is simply the process of moving an item from one place to another easily and quickly. It can be done easily with the use of the mouse or the touchpad of a laptop.

Most touchpads have two buttons located just below the touchpad itself that acts similar to the two buttons on the mouse pad. These two buttons might look like the real buttons on the laptop case, or just outside the touchpad, or on the touchpad itself. If that is the case, you might not notice they are there until you tap the lower-left corner or lower right part of the touchpad.

- Click on **the left button once or twice** to get just the same effect as though you were clicking the mouse the same number of times.

Dragging with a touchpad needs more skill than dragging with the use of a mouse.

You can **click twice and then slide your finger** to do just the same thing as dragging a mouse, or you can choose to hold down the left touchpad button with just one finger while the other finger slides or drags.

The mysteries of using a touchpad can take quite a while to get used to. It is best to add a mouse to the laptop to ensure you are not slow at the task you are trying to complete. It's best you learn how to make use of the touchpad though, as there might be a time when the mouse won't be available and the touchpad at that time will be a lifesaver.

Dispatching Tasks in a Flash

In the business world today, everyone seems to be doing less talking and more instant messaging and emailing. When your boss needs you to get certain things done, he most often communicates via email. The downside, though, to this is that all the messages can clutter the email box so quickly that you might lose track of what you are supposed to do.

Most productivity experts often propose that emails be converted into To-Do list items immediately after they're received. This way, you are sure you won't be losing track of important details. Make tasks from email messages by moving the messages to the Task label button located in the navigation bar. The other information, such as date and category, can then be added later. Note that a single move and drop is all that is needed.

Making Time Stand Still With Calendar Wizardry

The most common method of cheating plans with other people is the use of email. It is very cheap, fast, efficient, and reliable. It doesn't matter if you are including people at lunch, throwing a party, putting up a show, or arranging an exhibition, you must already have an idea of how easy doing all of these can be with the use of email.

When a plain email announcement about a certain event is received and you want to insert the details of the event into your calendar, you can do that in **Outlook by following the steps below;**

- Click **on the mail icon in the navigation bar** or make use of the keyboard shortcut by pressing the **Ctrl + 1 button to change to the mail module**. Once this has been done, a list of emails that have been received will be displayed.

- Choose **the message for which you want to make an appointment**.

- Move the message that you have chosen to the calendar in the navigation bar. An appointment form will then be opened with a text from the message that has been moved into the section bearing a note of the new appointment form.

- Perform any changes that should be added to both the start time and end time. This feature was made editable as the default start time might not be what you want.

- If there is a need to add more information about the event, enter the information in the appropriate box that can be found on the new appointment form.

- Once all of the above has been completed, click **on the "save and close" button**. This way, all the information regarding the event is now safely saved in your calendar for future reference.

The most amazing thing about creating an appointment from an email message is that all the details embedded in the message might just end up in your calendar. If there is a need for driving directions, agenda details, and any other information that was added in the message, simply double-click on the appointment in the calendar to get the details. If you use a smartphone with Outlook, such as an Android, Windows, or iPhone, all of the information on the Outlook calendar will be synced to your mobile device. With this, you are sure to have your appointment details with you wherever you go. If you are working with any organization that makes use of Microsoft Exchange for email, organizing meetings can be very easy as you can take advantage of certain features that are much more powerful.

Keeping Friends Close and Enemies Closer

You can move an email message to the People button in the navigation bar to create a contact record that also has the email address embedded in it. If this method is followed, the risk of misspelling the email address will be eliminated, and the work will also be saved.

To add a new contact from an email message, simply follow the steps below:

- Locate **the Mail module** > choose **the various messages to which a new contact record should be added**.

- Move the selected message(s) to the People button in the navigation bar. Once this is done, the new contact form will be displayed and will include the name and email address of the person who sent the message. Also, note that the original email sent will be displayed in the Notes area.

- If there is a need to add more information, enter the specific information into the relevant box on the new contact form. Existing information can be changed. You can also add more information such as the company the person is working for, the postal mail address, other phone numbers if available, and also personal details like if there is a need to send a complimentary gift, get the person a pet, and so on. If the body of the email message has certain information that can be useful as contact information, click **on that information** and move it to the necessary box of the New Contact form.

- Finally, click **on the "save and close" button**. Now you are certain that the email address and any other detailed information for the new contact have now been saved for future reference.

As an alternative, you can also capture an email address from an incoming message. This option seems to be very quick and much easier. To do this, simply **right-click on the name of the person** that sent the mail in the incoming message field (in the reading pane; note that this option will work if you right-click on the message from the message list). It may not seem like much, but right-clicking on it does. After this, a shortcut menu will be displayed. You can then choose the Add to Outlook Contacts option to open the New Contact Form and then follow the last two steps of the above-listed method.

Creating Instant Email Messages

Whenever an item is moved to the inbox, Outlook will immediately change it to an outgoing email message. If the item moved to the inbox has an email address, e.g., a contact. Outlook will automatically compose the message with the person's email address already filled in. If the item moved to the inbox has a subject, e.g. a task, Outlook will also create the message with the subject automatically filled in.

Creating an email from a name in your contact list

Having to add messages can be one of the most productive drag-and-drop operations in Outlook. Dealing with email addresses can be very difficult and tedious, and if by mistake, a letter from the email address appears missing, the intended message won't go through. The best approach to this is to keep the email address as a contact in the contact list of the people to whom you send email messages and also create new messages with the use of the email address.

To create an email address from the contact list, simply follow the steps below:

- Select people in the navigation bar to change to the People module. The contact list will then be displayed. You can choose to work with any view, but the address cards view is the easiest to work with. Click **on the first letter of the person's name to view the person's card**.

- Move a name from the contact list to the mail button in the navigation bar. This will then bring up the message form with the address of the contact filled in.

- Enter a **subject for the message** and ensure to keep it simple and straightforward; a few words will be enough.

- Select **the text box and enter your message**. There is also an option to change the text to bold, italics, or any other effect by choosing the necessary button located on the toolbar.

- Click on **the "send" button**. The display will then go back to the contacts list and the message will be sent.

Outlook Workspace Expansion

Views offer various ways an item can be seen in a given folder. Every folder in Outlook, like the inbox and calendar, offers users the opportunity to change the view and rearrange the way certain settings like fonts and others are organized.

One of the very common changes that can be made to a view is changing the size of the font in the reading pane and the message list or when composing a new message.

To change the font or font size in the messaging list, follow the steps below:

- Click on **the view option** >select **View Settings**.

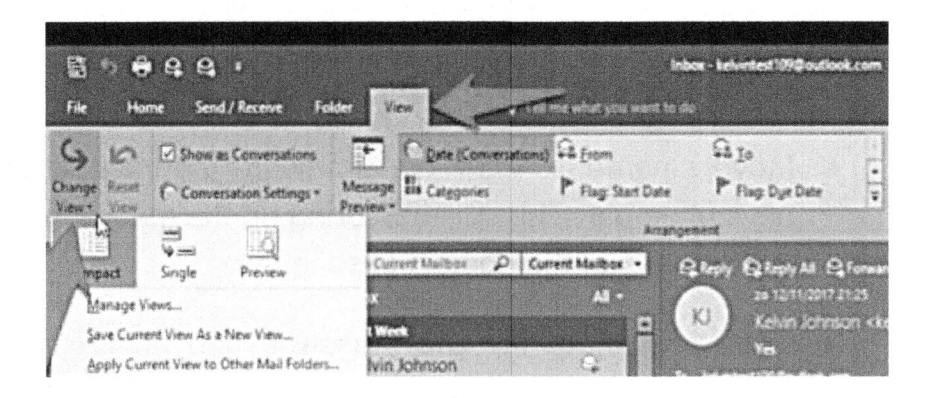

- Click on **other settings in the advanced view settings box**.

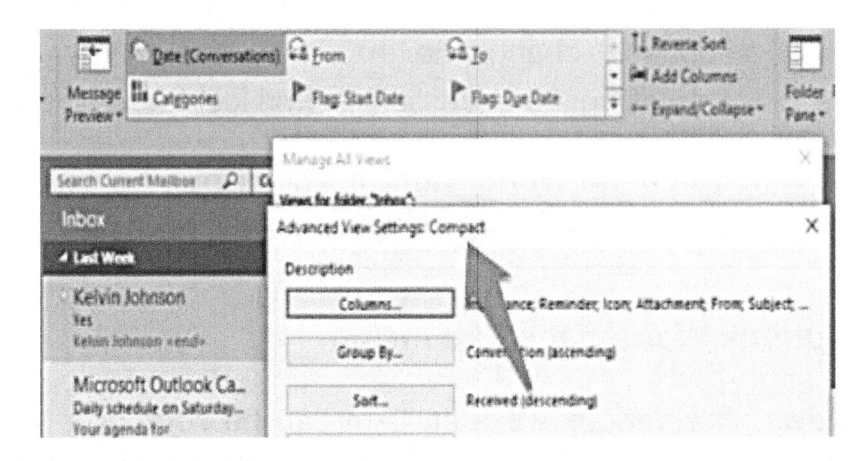

- Choose **the column font or the row font.** Note that to make changes to the size of the font in the message preview, the subject in the default inbox view, or the sender name, make use of the row font option.

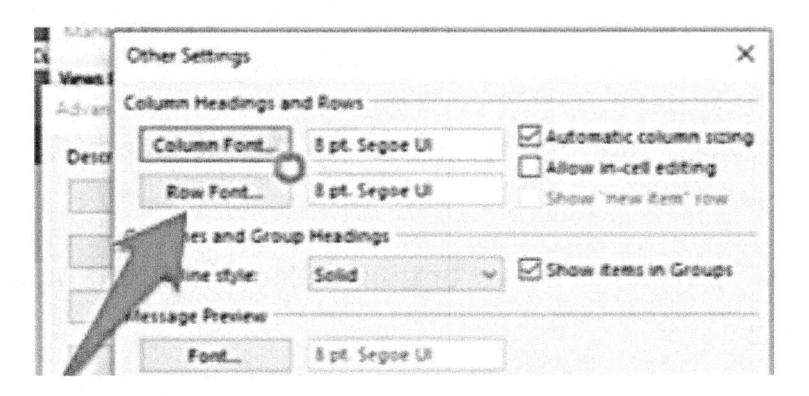

46

- Choose the **font, the actual font style, and the font size that you prefer**> click on **the OK button three times** to ensure the settings are saved and hence also applied. Take note: if all you want to change is the font or font size for the message preview (the line of the message text that can be seen beneath the subject and sender), click on the font beneath the message preview.

Changing the font or font size located in the reading pane

Outlook's reading pane will not allow you to make changes to the default font or font size. Nonetheless, there is an option to zoom out or zoom in with ease. There is also an option to command Outlook to show all of the email messages in plain text, and also take more control over the size of the font. On the other hand, Microsoft 365 subscribers (online version) can choose a certain zoom percentage that cuts across all of the messages read.

- Locate the lower right corner of the reading pane and choose the percentage (most times 100%) to show the zoom option when reading the dialog box.

- Select one **of the default percentages or insert the percentage of your choice**. Choose the **"remember my preference" option in the checkbox**. This way, the zoom level will be kept the same across all messages received.

To make changes to the zoom percentage, make use of the following steps:

If you want to zoom in or zoom out, find the magnification slider, which is located at the lower right corner of the reading pane.

Drag the slider to either left or right to make changes to the size of the text in the reading pane. Bear in mind that if any changes are made to the zoom level, they will only persist when the message is being viewed. If another message is chosen, the zoom percent will go back to 100. If you return to the initial message, the zoom percent won't be automatically saved.

Apply changes to the font size for messages when creating new messages, replying to messages, and forwarding messages.

To apply changes to the size of the font for messages when creating, replying, and forwarding, make use of the steps below.

- Click **on File>Options** > Mail, and then the Stationary and Fonts option.

- Choose **the font button for the New Mail Messages option** or the Replying or Forwarding message option to make changes to the default font, font color, and font size when creating or replying to messages.

- Finally, click **on the OK button twice** to ensure the changes are effective.

CHAPTER 4

THE ESSENTIAL SECRETS OF EMAIL

Email is very important for all professional communication in the office. If the organization you work with makes use of Outlook, learning how to make judicious use of it can be very vital to your professional development since the skills learned will help you arrange meetings with those you work with and also send email messages easily. Furthermore, you will be able to show your colleagues, boss, or team lead that you have learned well and improved over time when you make use of the features in Outlook with so much ease. You can even offer to teach them what they want you to know about the use of these tools.

Front Ends and Back Ends

There are basically two things needed to send and receive an email; a program that helps with the creation, saving, and management of messages and a program that actually sends the messages to people and also receives replies from them (exchanging messages). A few people in tech call these two parts the "front end" and "back end," as the case may be. Outlook, on the other hand, is a front end for email messages. It helps with the creation, formatting, storing, and management of messages, but it doesn't really do much about getting the message to the intended destination. Ensuring that messages get to their intended destination is the work of the back-end service (like the Microsoft Exchange Server in your office), the Internet Service Provider you use, and also by an online email service like outlook.com or gmail.com.

Email messages cannot be sent or received anywhere in the world without the use of an internet connection. The phone company you use most of the time provides internet services that can be used for this purpose. To ensure your email messages are sent quickly and you also get replies as quickly as possible, make sure you choose the best Internet Service Provider out there. Remember though, that the easiest choices aren't always the very best choices. There are several companies ready to offer internet services. Shop around to get the best value for money.

Creating Messages

In a lot of ways, electronic mail (email) is much better than the normal paper mail commonly known as snail mail. Email is delivered at a much faster pace (almost instantly) than paper mail. The speedy delivery can be of great help when closing a last-minute deal, sending across vital information towards the close of working hours, or for last-minute birthday greetings. Email is also very cheap to use; it is actually free most of the time.

The quick and dirty way

Creating a new email message can be very easy. Simply follow the steps below.

- Open Outlook The mail module will then be displayed, opening up the inbox.

- Click on **the New Email button**

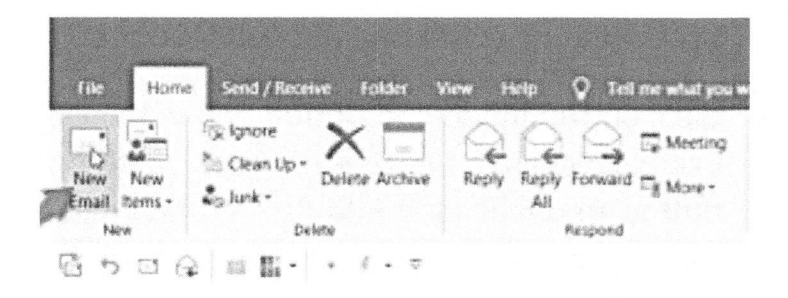

- Insert **an email address in the To box**.

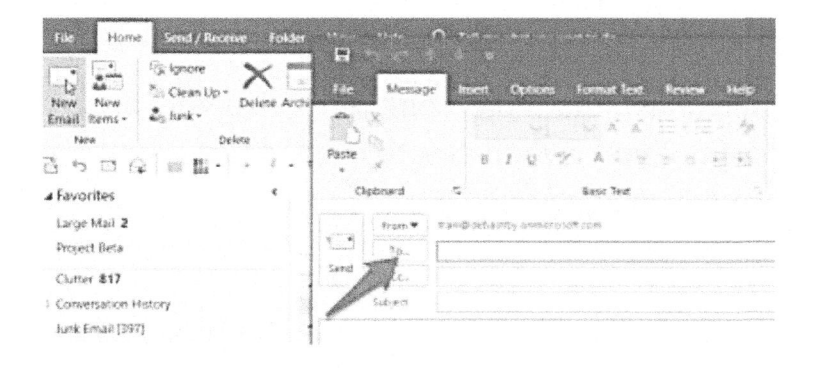

- Insert **a subject in the subject box.**

- Insert **a message in the message box**.

- And finally, click **on the send button**.

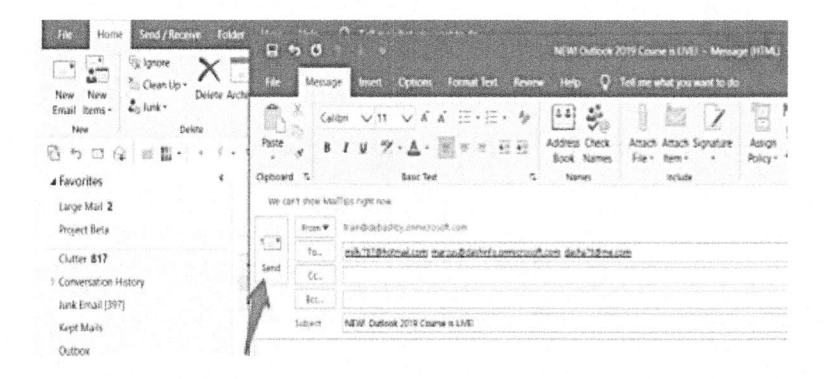

Most of the time, Outlook starts in the Inbox only. This will only change if the settings have been changed. If there is a need to start up in an entirely different folder than your inbox,

- Click on **the File tab and choose Options**.

- Click on **the advanced option** and in the Outlook Start and Exit part, change the Start Outlook. Click on **the "browse" button** to check all the folders in the Outlook data file. To begin in another module, select a folder that is similar to that module, e.g., Calendar or Notes.

The slow and complete way

You might like the more comprehensive way of creating an email message. If you love to create fancy emails, especially if you want to take advantage of every key feature Outlook has to offer, **follow the steps below:**

- Locate **the Mail module** > select **the New email button or press Ctrl + N**. The new message form will then open up.

- Click on **the "To" text box** and insert **the email address** of the person you are about to send a message to. If you are sending to more than one person, separate their email addresses with the use of either the comma or the semicolon. There is also an option of **clicking on the To button itself**, locating the names of the people you intend to send messages to in your address book, and **double-clicking on their names** to ensure they are added to the To text box.

- Click on **the Cc text box** and insert **the email address** of the person whom you would like to have a copy of the email message you are about to send. You can also click on **the "cc" button** to include people from your address book.

- Click on **the Check Names** option located on the New Message form's ribbon or press **the Ctrl + K button**. If you don't know the exact email address of those you want to send messages to, there is a feature known as "Check Names" that allows you to insert a portion of the address and then check it in the address book. Ensure to check what the feature enters to be double sure it is correct. There are times it will just automatically enter a similar name in the address book, which can lead to an embarrassing result if it is not corrected before the message is sent. An example would be a romantic message intended for your spouse being sent to your boss instead.

- Insert the subject of the message into the subject box. The subject should be very brief and simple, as it makes someone enthusiastic about reading your message rather than a very lengthy subject line. If for any reason, you forget to insert the subject, Outlook will open a window that asks if you really intend to send the message without a subject. Click on **the "Don't Send" button** to return to the message and include a subject. If there is really no need for a subject, click **on the Send button to send the message**.

- Type the body of your message in the message box. If Microsoft Word is the word processor you use, you must be familiar with the graphics table, modes of formatting, and all the tricks in Word to ensure your email appears more attractive. These very same tricks can be found in Outlook by making use of the tools at the top of the message form on the Format Text tab. There are times when you might not need to insert anything into the message textbox, like when you are forwarding a message or sending an attachment. If this appears to be the case, just skip this step and move on to the next.

Be extremely careful when formatting your email. This is because not all email systems can deal with graphics or text that has been formatted like boldface or italics. This way, the text you send to your client will not look like gibberish. Furthermore, most people read their email on phones or phablets, which can make the text you send look odd. If you are not certain about how your recipient will receive your mail, stay off of adding graphics or formatting text. You should only include them if you are very sure the recipient is also using Outlook.

- Click on **the Review tab** > select **the Spelling and Grammar** button at the upper part of the message screen. You can also choose to press **the F7 button**. Outlook will then run a spell-check to make sure your message is free of spelling and grammatical errors.

- Finally, click **on the send button** or press **Ctrl + Enter or Alt + S**. Outlook will then move your email to the outbox. If you are connected to the internet, Outlook will send any message in the Outbox immediately. If the message was composed when you were not connected to the internet, click the **F9 button** to send the message again when you are connected to the internet. When a message has been sent, it will move to the sent folder automatically.

Another option for telling Outlook to send messages from the Outbox is to tap the little button looking like two envelopes overlapping that can be found on the Quick Access Toolbar at the top left corner of the Outlook window, which can be seen from any module in Outlook. If the mouse pointer is moved over this button, a screen tip will be displayed notifying that it is the send/receive all folders button. Whenever messages are sent by clicking on the send button in a message or by tapping the F9 button, it is also a way of telling Outlook to receive all messages coming in.

Setting priorities

Certain messages can be more important than others. Sending a report to your boss is not the same as sending a friendly message to a teammate or colleague. Setting the importance level of a particular message to "high" informs the recipient that the message needs urgent attention.

There are basically three levels of importance you can choose from:

- Low
- Normal
- High

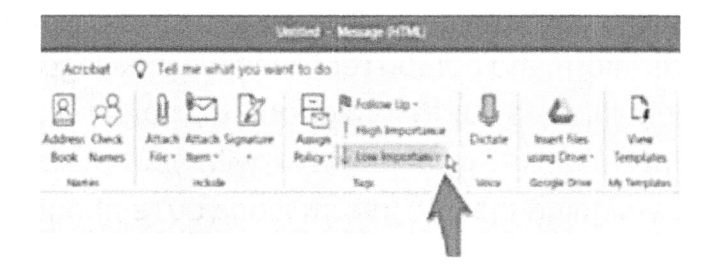

Setting sensitivity

There are times when there is a need for your message to be seen by only one person. Alternatively, you might just want to ensure your message is not altered by anyone after sending it. The sensitivity settings in Outlook help to put a restriction on what any other person might be able to do to your message after you have sent it. They also help you decide who that person can be.

In applying the sensitivity settings to a message;

- Click to **open the properties drop-down menu for messages**.

- Click on **the list box arrow closest to the word** "sensitivity" and any of the displayed levels as briefly described.

Most of the messages sent via Outlook have just the normal sensitivity, and this is what Outlook makes use of if the settings are not changed. Settings such as Private, Personal, and Confidential only inform those receiving the message that there might be a need to treat the message in a different way from the way they treat other normal messages. There are even certain organizations that employ the use of some strict measures in dealing with confidential messages.

Applying the sensitivity settings of a message to either private or confidential does not make it any different from other messages; all it does is inform the person receiving the message that the message has some information that might be delicate. If you use Outlook at work, make sure to double-check with your system administrators before assuming that the information you're about to send via email is secure.

Setting other message options

Upon clicking the Properties dialog box, you might see that there are quite a number of odd-sounding options. A few of these options are Request a Read Receipt for This Message (which informs you when the receiver reads the content of the message) and the Expires After option (this marks a message as expired if the receiver does not open the message before a stipulated time). These options are quite useful. The only glitch is that your email and that of the email receiver must support the setting, else it might not work. If both of you are on the same network, making use of the Microsoft Exchange Server, all should work just fine. If you are both not using Outlook or an Exchange Network, it can just be a gamble.

Adding an internet link to an email message

All Microsoft Office programs will automatically identify the address of certain things on the web. For example, if you insert the name of a certain webpage like www.facebook.com, Outlook will change the color of the text from black to blue and also underline the address, thus making it look like a hyperlink that is clicked on to move to another web page entirely.

This feature makes sending information about an exciting blog or website very simple; simply copy or type the address into your message. Note that Outlook might not identify the text as a web address if it does not start with "www." In that case, simply **add HTTP://** at the front of the text. Based on what the receiver uses in reading the email, he or she ought to be able to

simply **click on the text** and display a web browser forthwith, opening the page mentioned in the message.

Reading and Replying to Email Messages

Outlook has a number of methods to notify you when an email message has been received. The status bar located towards the left side of the Outlook screen will inform you of the total number of email messages you have in your inbox and the number of messages that are still unread. The word "inbox" will change automatically in the folder pane to a boldface form when there is an unread email. The titles of unread messages will also be bold.

To click open and read an email message, follow the steps below:

- Locate **the Mail Module**: click **on the title of the message you want to read twice**. This will open up the message in its window.

- Select **the close tab option (X)** or press **the escape key** to close the message pane when you are through.

Viewing previews of message text

At the time you begin to receive plenty of emails, some of them will be important, while others might not be very important, if not totally useless. Upon receiving the mail in your inbox, it can be very useful to know which is important and which is not. This way, you can focus on the very important one. You cannot depend on those sending the mail to tell you how important or otherwise it is. Outlook offers help by giving a glimpse at the first few lines of the message.

When launched, the message preview is always on and set to 1 line. This option can be changed to 2 or 3 lines, and you can also choose to turn it off totally. The Message Preview option becomes totally redundant if the reading pane is turned on, but if it is not, the preview can be a very useful feature.

To gain control over the previews of messages that have not been read, follow the steps below:

- Find **the Mail Module**>click on **the View tab option in the ribbon**.

- Click on **the Message Preview option**.

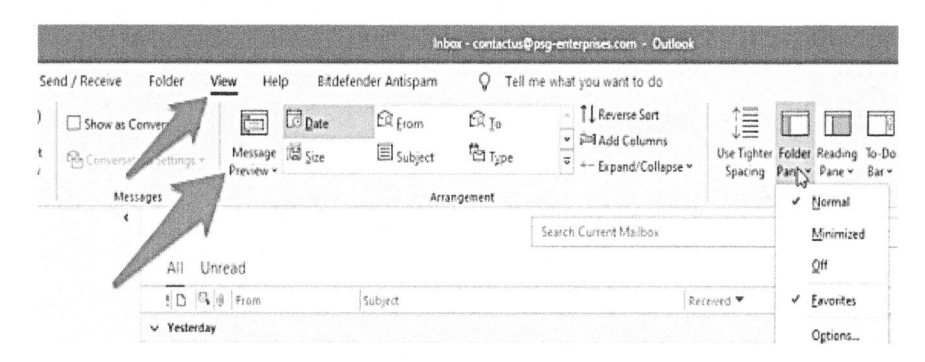

- Click on **the setting you prefer (1 line, 2 lines, 3 lines, or off)**.

- If, for any reason, there is a prompt to alter the settings found in all mailboxes or just this folder, select the option that works best for you.

All the modules in Outlook have a lot of viewing options that can be used to make information much easier to use. The Message Preview option is a very good way to scan through email if you don't want to make use of the reading pane.

Follow the steps below to set up the Reading Pane;

- Locate the **Mail Module** >click on **the View tab located on the Ribbon**.

- Select the **Reading Pane option**.

- Select from **the options on the right, bottom, or off**.

Either of the options you decide to choose, you cannot be wrong. You can also switch from one choice to another if the first choice chosen is not comfortable for you. When the reading pane is turned on, you can skim through it by using either the upward or downward button.

Sending a reply

One of the amazing benefits of using email is that replying to a message is very easy. There is no need to know the person's address when replying; just click **on the reply icon** and Outlook will sort the remaining.

To reply to a message, follow the steps below:

- Locate **the Mail Module**>select **the title of the message** that you want to reply to. If it is enabled, the selected message will be displayed in the reading pane.

- Select one of the options below

To reply to those located in the From Field, select the Reply button.

To reply to those in the CC field and the From field, select **the Reply All button**. A reply screen will then open in the reading pane area where the initial message was before. Email sent to a bunch of people can also be received at once. Ideally, it is expected that one person at the least will be named in the To field and more than one in the Cc field, which is for those you are sending just a copy of the email to. There is no need to keep replying to those in the CC field. You can also decide to reply to some of them if you wish.

- Enter **your reply** into the message box. Do not be dismayed if you find out that the message box already has some messages in it; they are part of the message that you are replying to. The cursor blinking will be in the upper part of the screen. With this, anything you type will appear before the other message. This means when you reply, the recipient can view the initial message to help refresh his or her memory about the discussion at hand.

- Select **the send button**, and your message will be sent with the message form disappearing and the message replying to reappearing.

- Press the **escape key** to close the message screen. This will make the message replied to disappear and the inbox will reappear.

Resending messages

Asking people to do just what you want is another amazing feature of email. Nonetheless, most people overlook things because they receive too much email. When you discover you are making the same requests again, it is high time you took advantage of the resend feature in Outlook. With this, there will be no need to type the original request again; just find the original message and send it again with a lovely reminder about when the initial message was sent.

To send a message again, follow the steps below:

- Locate **the Mail Module** and click on **the sent items folder in the folder pane**.

- Search for the message with the initial request and click **it twice**. This will leave the original message unopened. Doing this is essential because resending a message is not done from the reading pane.

- Select the **Actions Button located on the Message Tab** and then click on **the Resend This Message option**. This option will create a new copy of the former message automatically.

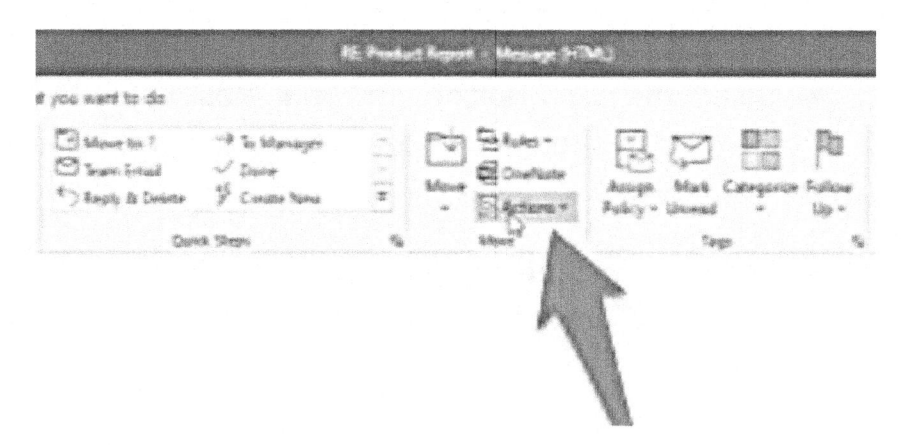

- Insert a reminder or make certain changes to the message if need be.

- Finally, click on **the "Send" button**.

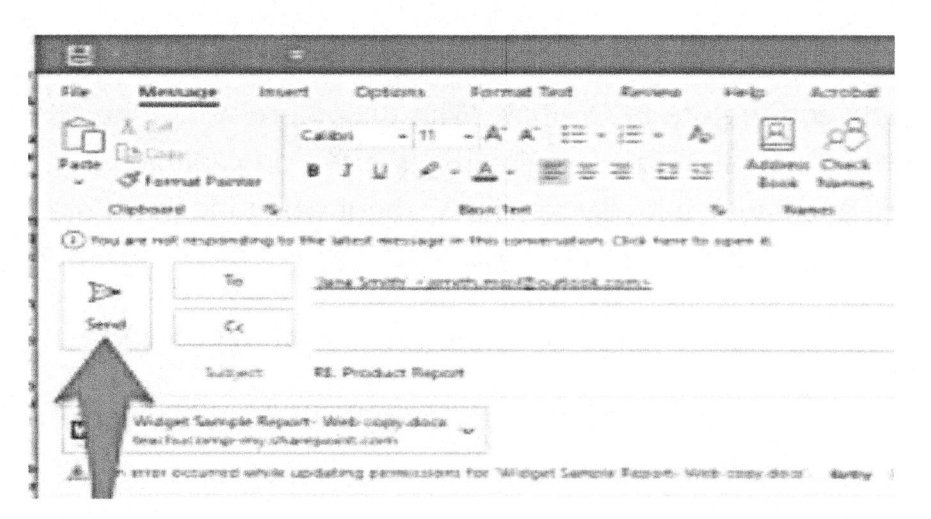

Don't get caught by phishing

Some cunning people are always looking to trick and deceive you, and most of the time, it is always on the internet. Recently, a very common scam known as "phishing" has caused people to lose their time and money, causing them grief after responding to an email from an impostor who makes a claim to be a representative of a bank or certain financial institution.

If you receive an email claiming to be from a bank or any other business and you are asked to click on a link for verification of your personal data, don't do it.

Oftentimes, the link will take you to a website that seems genuine, but the data you are asked to enter can be used for theft or fraud. Reach out to the organization directly to be sure the email isn't fake. If you are unsure of what to do, it is best to delete such an email.

If, on the other hand, you actually want to check in with the sender of the email, visit your browser and check out the organization's website if it is one you are quite familiar with. If the message looks very old, please do stay away from it.

That's not my department: Forwarding Email

When you don't have the answers to an email you received, you may need to forward it to someone else who can.

Follow the steps below to forward a message;

- Locate **the Mail Module**>select **the title of the message you intend to send**. The selected message will then be displayed in the reading pane.

- Click on **the Forward button**. The forward screen will then be opened, replacing the reading pane. The subject of the initial message will also be the subject of the new message, with the exception of the letters FW, which means forward and is entered at the beginning.

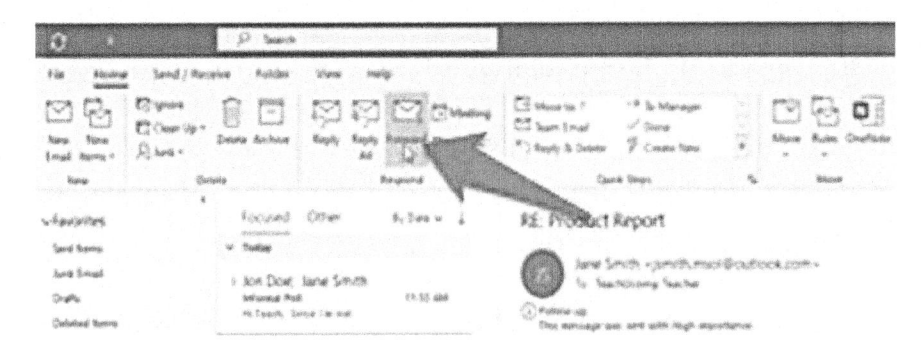

- Select **the To text box** and insert **the email address** of the person you intend to forward the message to. If the person is already in your address book, insert the person's name into the search box and Outlook will detect the email address.

- Select the **Cc textbox** and insert **the email address** of those you want to send a copy of the message to. A lot of people forward very trivial things to their colleagues via mail. A host of recipients are always added as cc addresses.

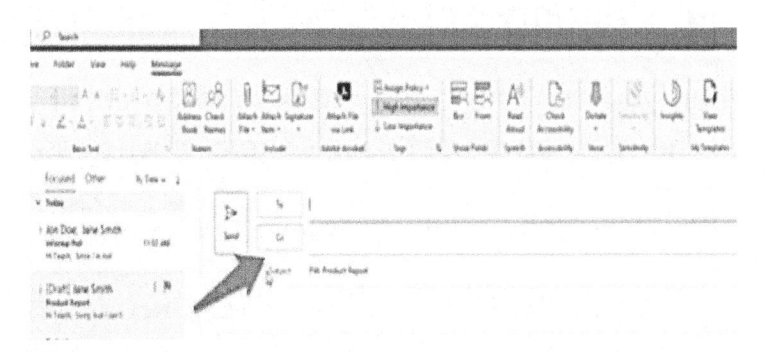

Blind Copying for Privacy

Whenever a message is sent to a very large group, all those who get the message can view the email addresses in the To and Cc fields. This means email addresses that some might want to keep private have just been given out. Everyone might have received too many bizarre, unsolicited messages before, and most of them will get peeved at the broadcast of their messages without their permission.

Blind copies offer the best of both worlds. If all the email addresses were inserted into the Bcc field, no one's privacy would be compromised. By making use of Bcc addresses, addresses that need to be kept secret can be kept secret.

Deleting Messages

It is possible to disregard an email message without having to think twice. There might be no need to read it at all. By taking a glance at the inbox list, you already have an idea of the sender and the content of the message. Hence, there is no need to waste so much time reading some unnecessary jokes. Simply take it off.

If by accident, a message you still need is deleted, to undo the action very quickly, simply press **the Ctrl + z button instantly**. If some other actions have been committed in error, click **on the Deleted Items folder in the Folder pane**; the messages that have been deleted in the past will be found there. To bring back a message that has been deleted, simply move it from the Deleted Items folder to the icon of whichever folder that it should be in.

To have a message deleted, follow the steps below:

- Locate **the Mail Module** > select **the title of the message** that should be deleted. It is not a must to read the message. You can delete it from the list immediately.

- Select the **Delete button** located on the Home tab on the Ribbon or simply click **on the Delete key** that is on the keyboard or press **the Ctrl + D button**.

The Delete button can be recognized easily; it is marked with a very big "X" sign, which simply means "Make this message disappear."

When messages are deleted, Outlook will not take off the deleted items; it simply drags them into the Deleted Items folder. (In some other mailing accounts and mail systems, it is known as trash rather than deleted items, though they mean the same thing.) If there are messages that have been unread in the Deleted Items folder, the name of the folder will be followed by the items that have not been read. It is possible to do away with the deleted messages forever by **right-clicking on the Deleted Items folder** located in the Folder pane and then **selecting an empty folder**. After the Deleted Items folder has been emptied, the messages in the folder will be gone forever.

Saving Interrupted Messages

If it happens that you get disturbed while composing an email, don't give up, as all is not lost. You can still get back to the mail. Whenever you begin to compose a message and then switch away to do other things without first sending the message, Outlook will save it automatically in the drafts folder.

To make sure it does this,

- Press the **Ctrl+S keys** before it saves automatically. When you are ready to continue working on the message being composed.

- Click on **the message and complete it by clicking on the send** button.

You can also click on the **"discard" button** if you decide not to continue with the message.

Saving a Message as a File

There are times you receive an email that is so wonderful or disheartening and you want to have the email saved. You can decide to either print out the message and show it to someone else, save the message to a disk, or simply send the message to a desktop publishing program.

To save a message as a file, go through the following steps:

- Locate **the Mail Module** with the message box open, choose **the File tab** on the Ribbon and then choose **the Save As Option or select F12**. This will open up the dialog box.

- Make use of the navigation pane located on the left side of the save as box to select the drive and folder in which the file should be saved. Outlook will at first choose the document folder by default, but there is an option to save the message on any drive and folder as it suits you.

- Select **the File Name text box** and insert **the specific name** you intend to give the file. Insert just any name you want. If you type a name that is not compatible with Outlook, it will bring up a window that states that the filename is not valid.

- Select the **triangle at the end** of the save as type box and select **text only as the file type**. There are various file options to choose from, but the text-only file format is the one that is read the most by other applications.

The various file type options are:

Text Only: This file format is very simple and easy to use in that it helps to remove all of the message formattings. As the name implies, only text messages are saved.

This is a format that is used to save messages that will be frequently used in Outlook. It helps to save not just message formatting but also attachments.

Outlook Message Format: This format ensures all message formatting and attachments are kept but can be read by Outlook only.

This is just the same as the former file format, but it makes use of the international characters that can be read by any version of Outlook that makes use of various languages. This is Outlook's default setting.

This helps to save a message in a file format option that can be shown in a web browser like Edge or Firefox. Or any application that can show HTM or HTML files. File attachments are basically not saved, although the message formatting is always kept. Furthermore, in addition to saving a copy of the message with the HTM file extension, another different folder is created which has the supporting files that the HTM file needs.

This is also known as the HTML file format; the only exception is that an additional folder is not created due to the fact that all of the content is saved in just one file. Applications that can show HTM and HTML files should also be able to show MHT files.

- Click on **the save button** and the message will be saved to the folder specified.

CHAPTER 5

EMAIL TOOLS YOU CAN'T DO WITHOUT

Outlook has the capacity to perform lots of tricks with the email messages that are sent out and the ones that are received. Messages can be flagged with reminders, customized with signatures, or have special formatting added to the messages sent as replies.

Nagging by Flagging

Over the years, flags have become the most used feature in Outlook. If you are the type that receives hundreds of messages daily and needs help with remembering those you need to reply to so that they won't get lost in the mix, it is best to flag that message as soon as it is read. This way, you are sure you will get back to the sender. A flag can also be planted in a message that you send to others in order to remind them of a particular task they have to carry out for you and the person on the other end using Microsoft Outlook.

One-click flagging

If flagging a message serves as a reminder of what needs to be done in relation to a specific message, you should be aware of the quickest way to do so.

When you move your mouse over any message in the inbox, towards the very end on the right side, a gray outline flag will be displayed, looking more like a shadow flag. When that shadow is selected, the color will change from gray to red, which means it has been flagged. When you then check through your list of messages, you can easily recognize the one that needs more attention. This way, the tracklist of flagged messages can be maintained even if they are below the bottom of the screen.

Once you have sorted the messages you flagged, click on the flag again. This will replace the flag with a checkmark indicating that the message has been taken care of.

Setting flags for different days

If you select a message once to include a flag, a copy of the message will be displayed in the task list, and various tasks scheduled for that day will also be displayed. There are times when you might not be in the mood to deal with certain messages. You might feel it is better to wait till the next day or the next week. All you have to do is

- Right-click **on the flag** and a list of possible dates for a flag will appear, including the next day, this week, next week, No date and customs will be displayed. Once a due date has been picked, it can still be changed if the need arises by moving the item from one due date to another with the use of the TO-DO bar. You can also choose to **double-click on the item** to have it reopened and then choose a different due date.

If the due date comes and goes and the flag remains unchanged, the message heading in the Inbox and To-Do bar will turn red.

Changing the default flag date

For those who are constantly busy or simply enjoy procrastinating, the default due date of flags can be changed by **following the steps below;**

- Click on **the "Follow Up" button** located in the Tags group on the Ribbon. This will then have the flag shortcut displayed.

- Select the **Set Quick Click** and a dialog box will be opened. The list in the box will provide different options for a due date.

- Lastly, select **the date that best suits you**. The date will then become the default flag due date.

If you have issues committing yourself to a certain date, choose the "No Date" option and wait until someone raises an alarm.

Adding a flag with a customized reminder

Without a doubt, flags can actually do a whole lot more than just stand for a week or more. Flags in Outlook can pop up as a reminder, reminding you of what needs to be done. Flags can also be used to pester someone else when a reminder is attached to a message sent to someone else. Adding a reminder to a flag cannot be completed with a single click.

Follow the steps below to do that;

- Locate **the Mail Module** and right-click **on the message that needs to be flagged**. The flag shortcut menu will then be displayed.

- When this is done, the custom dialog box will then open up and if you click **on the OK button** at this point, the message will be flagged and ready for a reminder at 4 pm. This reminder can be adjusted, especially if the time is too close.

- Select the **list box arrow** at the right side of the Flag to Text box and click **on one of the menu items.** A handy flag means "Follow Up" and reminds you to affirm a certain arrangement or appointment, as the case may be.

- Insert the **dates in the Start Date box**, Due Date box, or all of the boxes. The date and time inserted will determine when a reminder will pop up to help jog the memory of the appointment. Ensure the dates are typed in a way Outlook will remember.

- Click on **the OK button**. Once the reminder date that has been entered into the custom dialog box is up, the reminder dialog box will then help to offer a nudge.

Changing the date on a reminder

Don't get nagged with a reminder; you can always pull it off and do it much later.

To change the date on a reminder that was sent to you by someone else, follow the following steps:

- Locate **the Mail Module** and select **the message that has the reminder that needs to be changed**. The message will be displayed as highlighted when it has been selected. To open the custom dialog box, simply right-click **on the message**.

- Click on **the Home tab** and select **the Follow Up on the Ribbon option**, then include a reminder. As an alternative, press **the Ctrl+Shift+G buttons**.

- Click on **the Reminder checkbox** and, if it has not yet been selected, choose **a new date for the reminder flag to show up**. If the checkbox has already been selected, leave it as if you click **on it again**, it will then leave it deselected.

- Finally, click **on the OK button**.

There is also an option to click **on the snooze button** in the reminder dialog box to turn off the reminder flag for some time when it pops up, the same way it is done with the alarm clock.

Saving Copies of Your Messages

There is nothing handier than having to know what has been sent and when exactly it was sent. All outgoing email messages in Outlook can be saved. This way, you can always go back and check the message that has been sent. Immediately after the Outlook program is installed on a computer, it starts saving sent messages. This feature can, however, be turned off. Before attempting to do so, check your message folder to be sure it contains sent messages.

To save copies of the messages, simply follow the steps below.

- Choose **the File tab** > select **the Options button**. This will then open up the Outlook dialog box.

- Select **the Mail button** and locate **the navigation window on the left side**. The mail settings will then be displayed.

- Move down to the Save Messages section and click **on the Save copies** of the messages in the Sent Items folder check box if it hasn't already been selected.

- Then finally click **on the OK button**.

Setting Your Reply and Forward Options

The look of a forwarded message can be controlled as well as the replies. If you use Microsoft Outlook, your text can be made to look really incredible in your messages by the addition of graphics, special effects, or some wild-looking fonts. If mail is being sent to people who use other programs and not Microsoft Outlook or to those using web-based email services like Gmail, some of the effects might not be well translated.

To set your options, follow the steps below:

- Click **on the File tab**, locate **the ribbon**, and click **on the Options icon**. The options dialog box for Outlook will then open up.

- Select the **Mail button** located in **the navigation window** on the left side and the mail settings window will then be opened.

- Move downwards to the Replies and Forwards section and select **the list box arrow** at the right side of the Reply to a Message box. A menu of options will then be displayed, including the original text as the default option. The diagram located on the left side of the menu will show how the message will be displayed when each option is chosen.

- Select **the preferred style** to use for replying to messages. A little diagram on the left side of the menu will change instantly to display what your choice will look like. You can try another if you don't like the choice you made earlier.

- Click on **the list box arrow** that can be seen on the right side of the When Forwarding a Message box. This menu option looks almost the same as the one above, with just one fewer choice.

- Select **the style preferred** to be used for forwarding messages.

- Click on **the OK button**. The Outlook Options dialog box will then be opened.

By making use of Outlook, there is so much room to explore and do all sorts of fancy and even useful tricks with email. If the advanced options menu appears confusing, you can easily ignore them and just click on **the Reply button** and insert **your reply**.

You can also choose to delete the original message when a forward is created or replied to, but it's best to include at least a part of the original message. This way, it will make the response easier to understand. There is also an option to choose and delete some parts of the main text that are not relevant to your reply.

Adding Comments to a Reply or a Forward

When a message is forwarded or replied to, it is okay to type the reply above the original message if the original is short and simple. But if the original message is quite complicated and embedded with so many questions, it is best to type the reply in the original message, replying to each question as it appears.

The only issue that might arise with typing replies within the original message is that it is not always very clear what the format of the new reply is and the original message. To sort that out, Outlook provides a means by which you can preface any in-line replies that are being made with your name or whatever is needed. This also makes the reply text bold and clear, making it stand out more.

To include the in-line replies with your name, go through the steps.

- Click on **the File tab located on the Ribbon** and select **the Options icon**. The Outlook Options box will then open.

- Select **the mail button** located in the navigation window on the left side to open the mail settings window.

- Move downwards to the Replies and Forwards part and choose the **"Preface comments with the checkbox.**

- Within the preface comments, With the text box, enter **the text you deem fit** to be used as the prefix to all of the text that will be typed whenever you reply to messages.

- Finally, click **on the OK button**.

Sending Attachments

If you have created a document in another application and you don't want to send it just yet, there is no need to type the same message all over again in Outlook; simply **send the document as an attachment to an email message**. Word processing documents, spreadsheets, and other presentations such as PowerPoint can all be attached. You can also choose to include pictures and music; any type of file can be sent as an attachment.

The Send From menu is the simplest way to send a file from a Microsoft Office program such as Microsoft Word.

- Open **up the file in the program it has been created in.**

- Choose the **File tab option** located on the ribbon.

- Select the **"share" button**.

- Choose the Word document from the share dialog box and write the message in Outlook.

If you don't want that option, you can have a message sent directly from Outlook by following the steps below.

- Locate **the Mail Module** and select **the New Email button** that can be found on the Ribbon. You can also press **the Ctrl + N button** if you prefer to use a shortcut.

- Choose **the Attach File button found** on the New Message form's Ribbon.

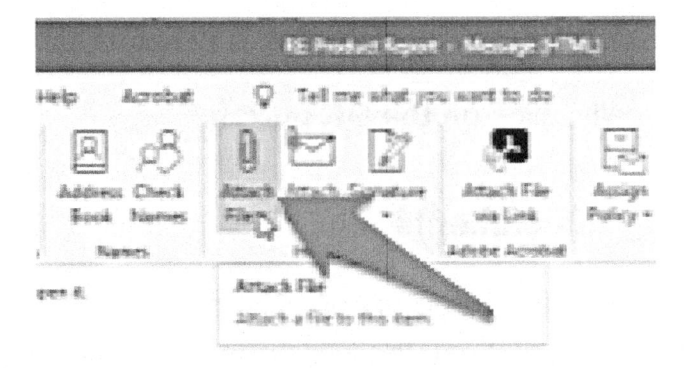

A list will then drop down to display the names of the files that have recently been worked upon.

You may be lucky enough to find the name of the file there, then just **click on it.** If the name of the file is not there, select

the Browse This PC option located at the lower part of the screen. This will then open up the Insert File Dialog Box.

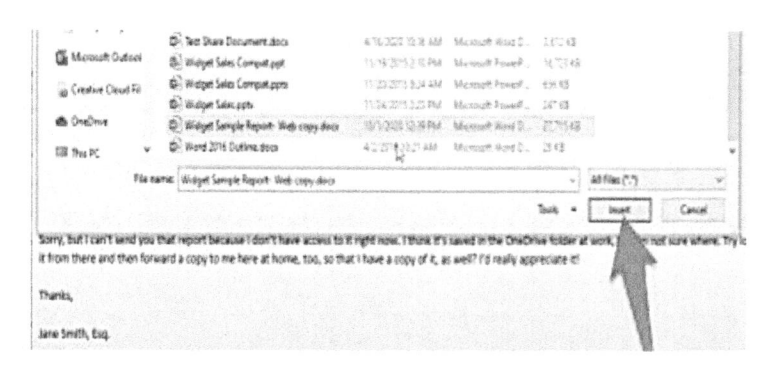

Click **on the name** of the preferred file and tap the send button. The name of the file will then be displayed in the Attached box in the message form's message header. When the email message is sent, a copy of the selected file will be sent to the recipient.

- Enter a message if you have one to send. There might be no message and you just want to send an attachment. Take note that the content of the attachment will not be displayed on the screen of the recipient until the attachment is opened.

- Click on **the "To" button** in the message form. The dialog box for choosing names will then be displayed.

- Choose **a name** from the contact list and click **on the button in the Select Names dialog box**. This will then open up the name of the person that has been selected. This process can be repeated if you want to include more than one recipient.

- Select **the OK button**. The name of the person can now be found in the To box of the message.

- Click on **the Subject text box** and insert **a subject for the message**. The option of a subject is not compulsory, but if you want the message to look important, a subject can be helpful.

- Finally, click **on the "send" button**.

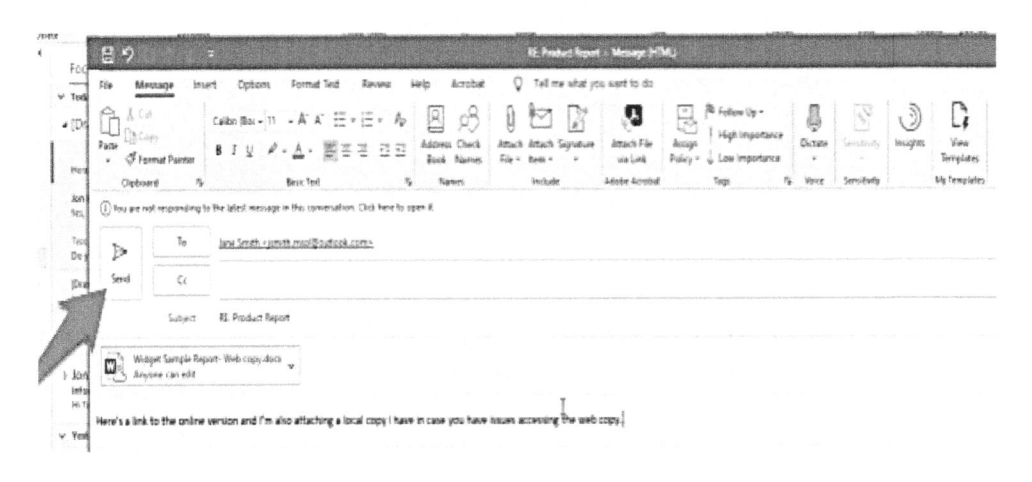

Emailing Screenshots

It is often said that pictures are worth more than a thousand words. Most of those words become four-letter words when the computer begins to act up. This makes it very difficult to describe the type of problem in an accurate manner. When problems like this arise, Outlook can be of help.

A screenshot is simply a picture of the screen of a computer that is captured to show what is being done on the computer at that point in time. This ebook contains lots of screenshots to make certain steps and procedures more comprehensible. The exact same thing can be done with the screenshot feature in Outlook. A screenshot can be sent to help a person solve a problem with his or her computer. A screenshot can be sent off just about anything, including pictures and documents. The possibilities of this feature are endless.

To include a screenshot in an email message, simply follow the steps below.

- When an email message or a reply is being composed, select **the Insert tab on the ribbon**. If you notice the screenshot button is grayed out, ensure the cursor is inside the body of the email message.

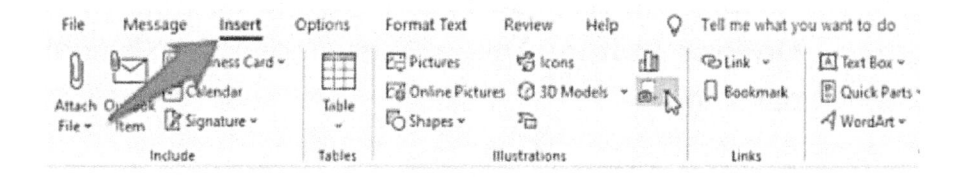

- Tap **the screenshot button**. This will then display a gallery of thumbnail images.

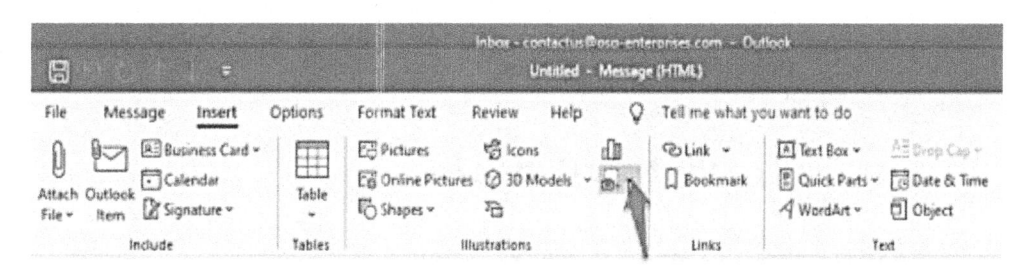

- Choose **any one of the screens from the gallery**. The screenshot that has been chosen will then be displayed in the body of the email message.

- Conclude **with your email message and send it to the recipient**.

Creating Signatures for Your Messages

Most people love to include signatures at the very end of the messages they send. A signature, most of the time, is just a few lines of text that show you to all those that read your message and also states certain things you want them to know. Lots of people include their names, the names of their businesses, and also the web addresses, their motto, and a little personal information. You can set Outlook to automatically include a signature in all outgoing messages, but a signature file must be created first. To create a signature

- Choose **the File tab found on the Ribbon** > Click **on the Options button**. This will then open the Outlook Options dialog box.

- Select **the Mail button** in the navigation window towards the left side. This will open up the Mail settings window.

- In the Compose Message section, click **on the signature button**. The signature and stationery dialog box will then be open.

- Click on **the New Button icon**.

The dialog box for a new signature will open.

- Enter **a name** for the new signature. The name that is typed will then be displayed in the New Signature box.

- Click on **the OK button** to complete this process. The dialog box for the new signature will then close.

- Enter **the text of the type of signature** that you prefer in the Edit Signature box and include any formatting that suits you. To apply changes to font, color, size, or other text characteristics, make use of the button in the text box. You can choose to make the signature in Word and then copy and paste it in the Edit Signature box.

CHAPTER 6

DEALING WITH MESSAGES

Most people spend a lot of time on email messages. Some experts also estimate that an average business employee spends about 2 hours per day on emails. Very soon, more time will be spent on email than on actual work.

Outlook has some tools for dealing with the influx of flotsam and jetsam that finds its way into your message inbox. Different folders can be created for filing mail, and you can also make use of Outlook's View feature to help slice and dice incoming messages into smaller groups. Old messages can also be archived to save your inbox from becoming cluttered.

The Rules Wizard is even considered a better feature than the View feature. The Wizard responds to messages coming in just the way you want. All messages can also be moved from specific senders to the folder you choose.

When talking about spam, the use of junk email filters in Outlook is a better way to deal with aggressive or offensive messages. Ensure the filters are turned on already. You can also crank up the settings so that there will be less junk mail cluttering the message inbox.

Organizing Folders

By now, you are most likely used to arranging items into folders. Windows helps to arrange all the other documents into folders. Outlook will also do the same. Simply create a folder and move your stuff into it.

Creating a new email folder

The simplest and easiest way to cope with messages coming in is simply to file them. Before a message can be filed, at least one folder wherein the file will be stored will be created. The folder is there for life unless you decide it is no longer needed and you delete it. You can create as many folders as you need.

To create a folder, simply follow the steps below:

- Locate **the Mail Module** and choose **the inbox option in the folder** pane or press **the Ctrl + Shift + I buttons**. If you were not doing some other thing before, the inbox should be selected by default when Outlook is opened.

- Choose **the Folder tab** and select **the New Folder button located on the Ribbon**. This will open the Create New Folder dialog box.

- In the Name text box, enter **a name** for the new folder. You can choose to use any name that suits you. You can also make as many folders as possible. There shouldn't be too many folders either, to avoid confusion.

- Click on **the OK button**. The new folder will then be displayed in the Folder pane.

Moving messages to another folder

Filing messages can be as easy as moving them from the folder they are into another folder where you prefer them to be. All you need to do is open the box when they arrive and move each message to the folder where you want it. For another method of moving the messages to a different folder, **follow the steps below:**

- Locate **the mail module** > click on **the title of the message** that should be moved. The message will then be highlighted.

- Choose **the Home tab option** and click **the Move button on the ribbon**. The move drop-down menu will then be open.

- Choose **the name of the preference folder** to which the message should be moved.

Organizing Your Email with Search Folders

The search folders feature in Outlook was created to help arrange messages in the inbox and in other folders. The Search Folder offers one space where a specific type of message can always be found. A search doesn't move messages; it just creates a kind of an imaginary location for messages. This way, you only have to look at one type of message at a time.

When Outlook is initially opened, search folders are not displayed in the folder pane. If there is a need to use search folders, there will be a need to include one of the default search folders or make a search folder of your choice.

Setting up a search folder

To set up a search folder, follow the following steps:

- Locate **the Mail Module** and select **the inbox** to choose the folder in the Folder pane.

- Choose the Folder tab and then select the New Search Folder button located on the Ribbon. As an alternative, you can also press **the Ctrl + Shift + P buttons**. This will open the New Search Folder dialog box.

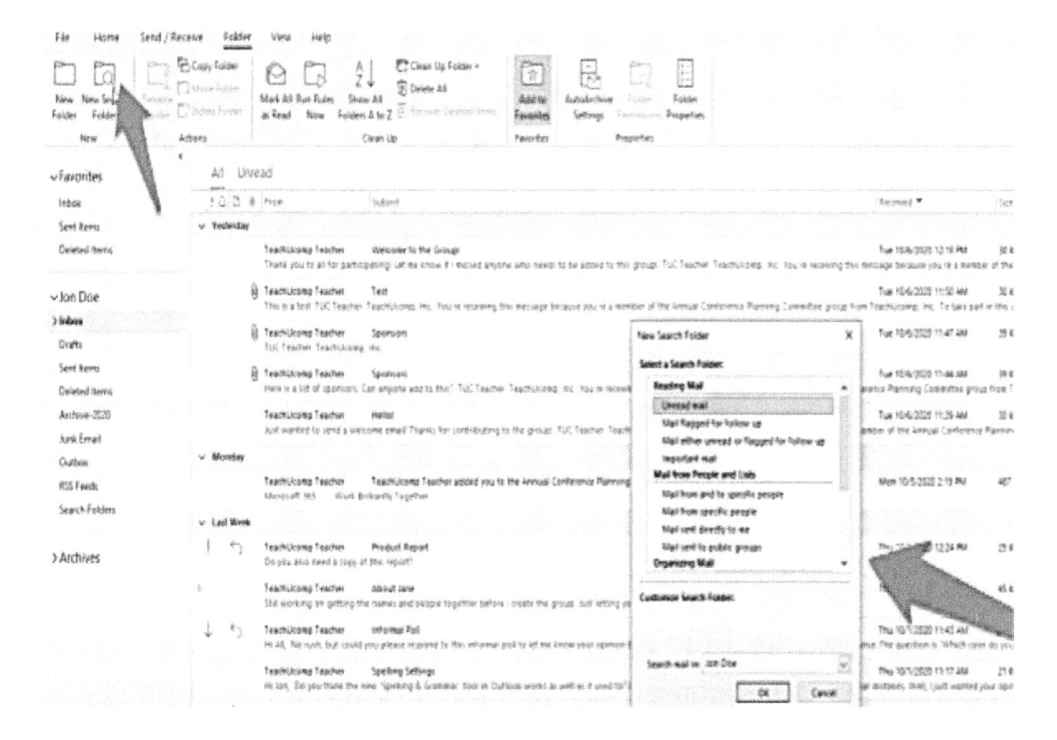

- Choose **the type of search folder** that should be added from the list in the New Search Folder dialog box. Lots of folders are available and will be displayed. You can choose to use an existing folder or create a folder of your choice.

- If a button showing "Choose" is displayed in the lower part of the New Search Folder dialog box when you click on a search folder, click on **the button** and enter **the information requested**.

- Click on **the OK button** and the New Search Folder dialog box will be closed, displaying the new search folder in the navigation pane.

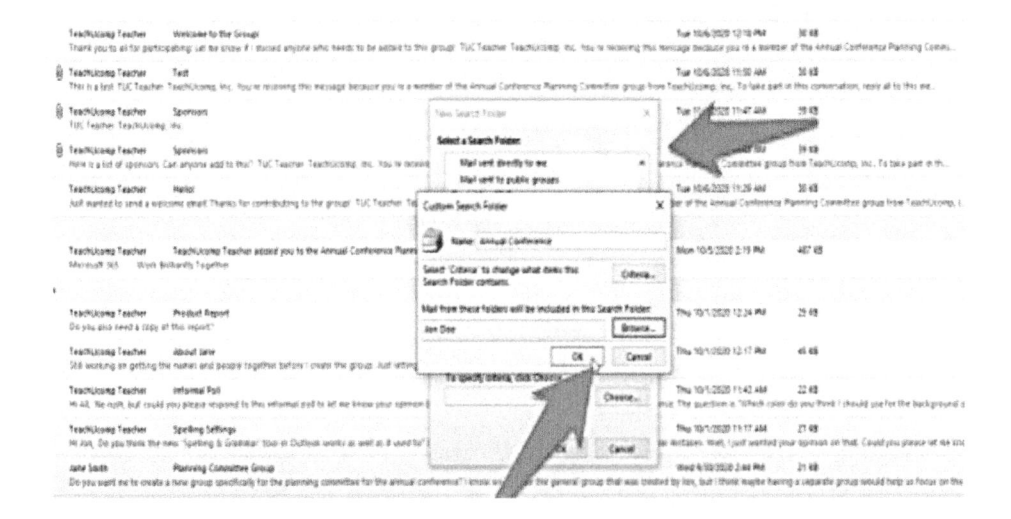

Some very useful predefined folders include:

Email marked for Follow up: This folder displays messages that have been flagged only. When the flag is removed from a particular message, it will no longer be seen in this folder but can still be found in the inbox or any folder it primarily is.

Large Mail: This folder arranges messages by the amount of storage space they need. Normally, you aren't concerned with the amount of storage required by messages you receive but don't be surprised if the system administrator where you work insists on not storing too many messages. If you have lots of messages that include attachments, your inbox might get filled up quickly.

The large mail folder can be used to discover the messages taking up so much space and delete the largest ones. The messages that will be displayed in the large mail folder will be characterized by size, beginning with "large," then "huge," and "enormous."

Unread Mail: This folder displays only unread messages. When a message in this folder is read, it leaves the folder, but it will still be displayed in your inbox.

Using a search folder

There is no need to do anything special to make use of a search folder. Simply

- Click **the name of the preferred search folder** that you want to search for in the Folder pane, and a list of those kinds of messages will be displayed.

When you are set to get back to your inbox,

- Click **on the inbox button** located in the folder pane to view the collection of all the messages again.

Deleting a search folder

Once the search folder has served its purpose, there is no need to keep it again.

You can delete the search folder by:

- Locate **the Mail Module in the Folder pane** > right-click **on the search folder** that should be deleted.

- Click on **the Delete Folder button**.

- Choose **Yes**. The search folder will then disappear.

Using the Reading Pane

If all you want to do is skim through your bunch of messages swiftly, the reading pane can be of great help. The reading pane is shown by default in Outlook. If somehow it gets closed,

- Click **on the View tab option**.

- Select **the reading pane located on the ribbon**.

- Click **on the right icon to then open it**.

When the reading pane is fixed to the right, the inbox screen will then show a list of messages on the left of the center of the folder pane is shown and the content of the chosen message is also on the right side.

When you want to move from one message to the other, press the upward or downward arrow key. Messages can also be viewed in the inbox when the message title is selected. If you wish to have the message displayed on the lower part of the screen instead,

- Select **the "View" tab option**.

- Choose **the reading pane button on the ribbon**

- Click o**n the bottom option**. Note that you won't be able to see many messages using this method. It is best to set the reading pane to show on the right side.

The reading pane shows a lot more message content than when the message preview option is used. If you receive messages that have formatting or images, the graphical view will be better appreciated when the message is viewed in the reading pane.

Playing by the Rules

Rules are just another of the amazing features in Outlook. This feature helps you make Outlook act on a specific type of email message automatically. For example, if you get lots of messages that can easily waste your time when you are trying to sort them, you can simply set up rules in Outlook to sort incoming mail into various folders. There are so many rules that can be created with the use of the Rules Wizard.

Creating a rule

There comes a time when you will discover the need to make a rule. By making a rule, you can set those you want to read their messages and avoid reading some mail that might make you feel bad or set the day on a bad note for you.

The Rules Wizard is termed a "wizard" because of the way the feature leads you to create each rule step-by-step. The process can be very simple.

To create a rule to move a message coming in from a particular person to a specific folder, follow the steps below:

- Locate **the Mail Module** and choose **the inbox icon** located in the Folder pane.

- Move to the home tab located on the Ribbon and select **the Rules button** > Click **on the Manage Rules and Alert option**. Do not click on the option to "Create a Rule" on the Rules button's options menu, as the options will be limited based on the message that is currently selected. Choosing Manage Rules and Alerts will open the Rules and Alerts dialog box, though you will still be just a click away from the Rules Wizard.

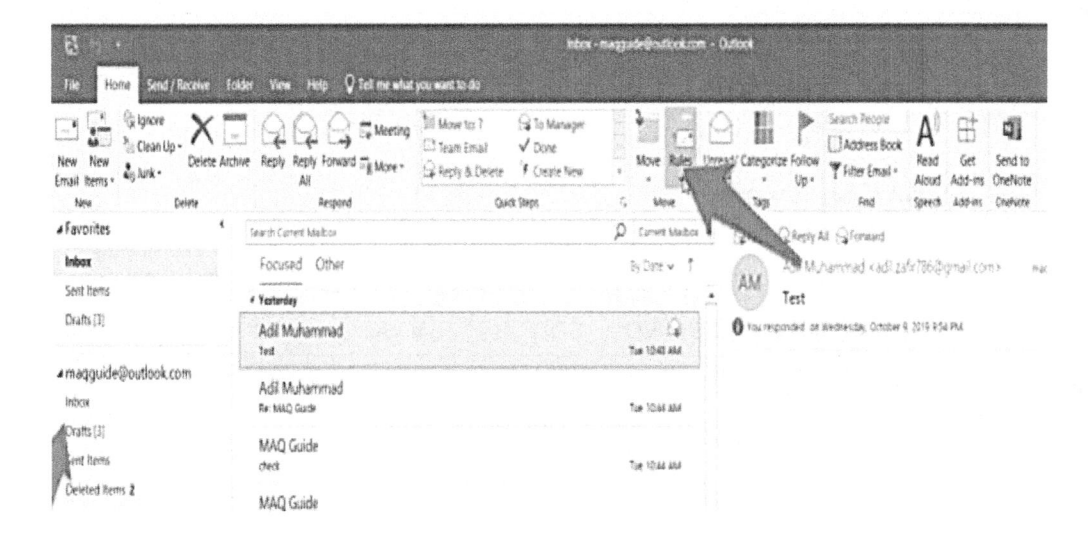

- Select **the Create Rule button**. This will then open the Wizard dialog box, which has a list of the types of rules you can make.

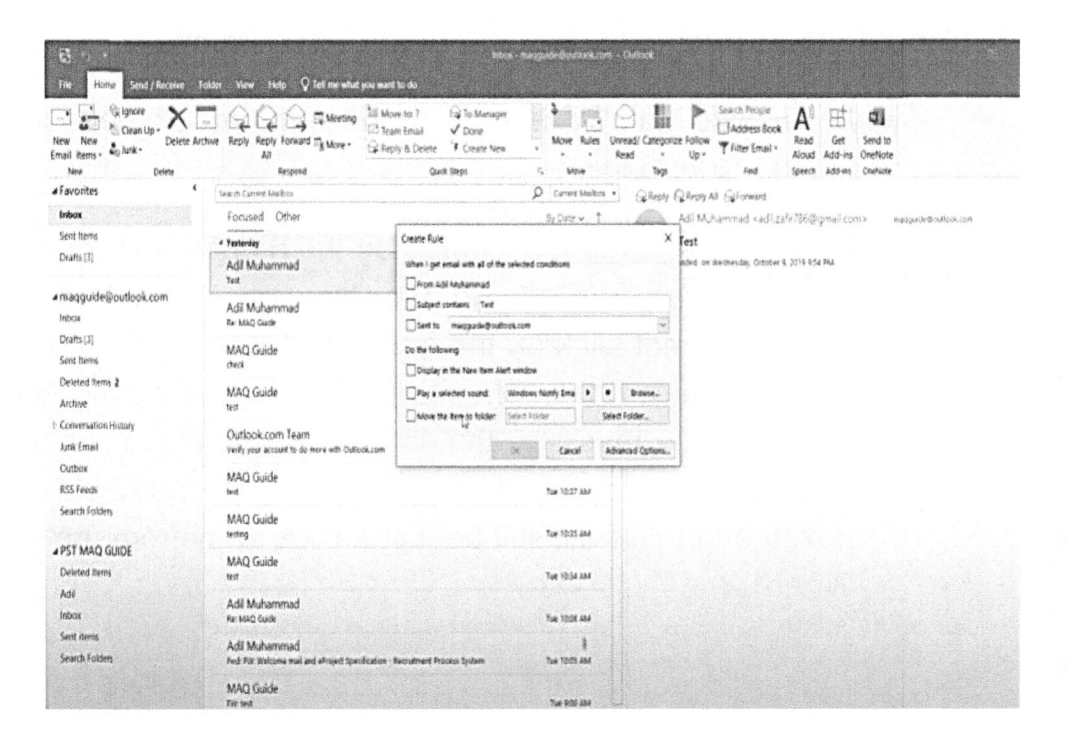

Select the type of rule you want to make.

The Rules Wizard provides various common types of rules you might want to make, like:

- Drag messages from a person to a folder.
- Drag messages with a certain type of word into the subject folder.
- Drag messages that were sent to a public group to a specific folder.

The collection of suggested rules is split into useful groups like "Stay Organized" and "Stay Up to Date." When you have made your choice, click on the Next button, and then you will see a message in the rule description box.

- Locate **the select conditions box**, ensure that the From People or Public Group selection has a checkmark sign at the front of it, and click on the first piece of text underlined in the rule description box which says People or Public Group. This will then open the Rule Address dialog box.

- Click twice **on the names of each of the people** whose messages should be moved to another folder. The email address of each of them will then be displayed in the From text box at the lower part of the Rule Address dialog box.

- Once all the people whose messages should be moved have been chosen, click **the OK button**. This will then close up the Rule Address dialog box and the names of the people that have been chosen will be displayed instead of "people" or "public group" in the rule description box.

- Choose **the next piece of text underlined** in the rule description box that says specified. This will open a dialog box providing you with a choice of folders that the messages can be moved to.

- Click twice **on the name of the folder** in which you want to move the messages. This will close the dialog box and the name of the folder that has been selected will appear in the sentence in the rule description box. More rules can be added by **choosing them from the Select conditions box**. If the next button is selected a few more times, actions like clearing the message flag and exceptions like "except if sent to me alone" can be added to your rule.

- Click **on the Finish button**. This will open up the Rules and Alerts dialog box again, offering a list of all the rules. Each rule has a check box next to it, and by selecting or deselecting the checkbox, you will either turn on or off the rules. If a checkmark is shown next to the rule, it means it is turned on and, if otherwise, it means it is turned off.

- Select **the OK button** to have the Rules and Alerts dialog box closed.

Rules can do a lot more than just sort messages that are coming in. Rules that can reply automatically to certain messages, flag messages with a specific word in the subject, and also have messages from certain people deleted can be created.

Putting a rule into action

Immediately after messages enter the inbox, rules swing into action. When a rule to move messages from a particular person to a specific folder is created, the message that arrives after that rule must have been created will move automatically, but the messages that were already in the inbox before the creation of the said rule will remain in the inbox.

If you want the rule to affect the messages already in the inbox, follow the actions below.

- Locate **the Rules and Alerts dialog box** and choose **the specific rule** you want. If the Rules and Alerts dialog box is not already open, click **on the Rules button** located on the Home tab of the Ribbon and then click **on Manage Rules and Alerts**.

- Select **the Run Rules Now icon** located at the top of the dialog box. The dialog box for the Run Rules will now be opened.

- Select **the name of the rule** you want to run and place a checkmark near it.

- Choose **the "Run Now" button**. The Rules and Alerts dialog box is currently covering the screen; hence, the result of the rule cannot be seen yet. Once **the close button and OK button have been selected**, it will be obvious that the rule has already been carried out.

Filtering Junk Email

Are there times when you feel overwhelmed by the influx of junk email in your inbox? You are not alone. Lots of junk email is now being sent over the internet instead of genuine ones. Outlook has a feature that checks all your incoming messages and moves the ones that look like junk email (spam) automatically to a special folder. Anything that gets moved into the junk folder can be immediately deleted over and over again after you must have checked to be sure that Outlook has not made a mistake in moving a real email to the junk folder.

There is just no such thing as a perfect machine, and there is no program running on a machine that can be perfect. This means Outlook can make certain mistakes when catching junk mail, but it can still be relied upon. Some people, however, prefer to make use of software that works with Outlook to sieve out junk mail.

Fine-tuning the filter's sensitivity

Based on your settings in Outlook, automatic filtering might be on already and probably set to low, or it might as well be turned off. The low setting is somewhat conservative, looking for the most visible spam but not stopping most emails from entering is at least kind of plausible as legitimate mail. The high setting can be very aggressive and sometimes takes off messages you want to see. To make some changes to Outlook's junk email settings, follow the steps below:

- Find **the Mail Module** > click **on the Home tab** > select **the Junk icon** in the Delete group located on the Ribbon

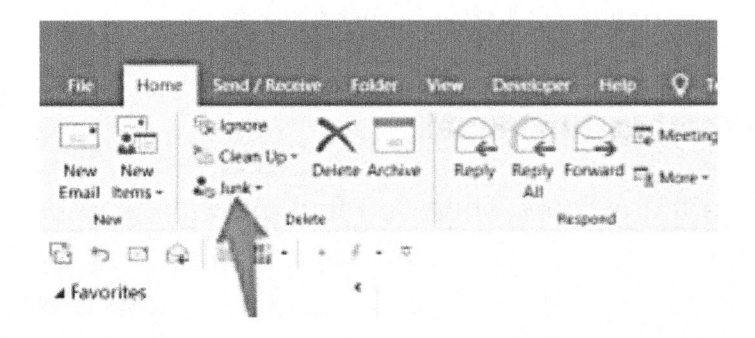

Choose **the Junk Email Options.** This will open up the Junk Email dialog box with the Options tab placed at the top.

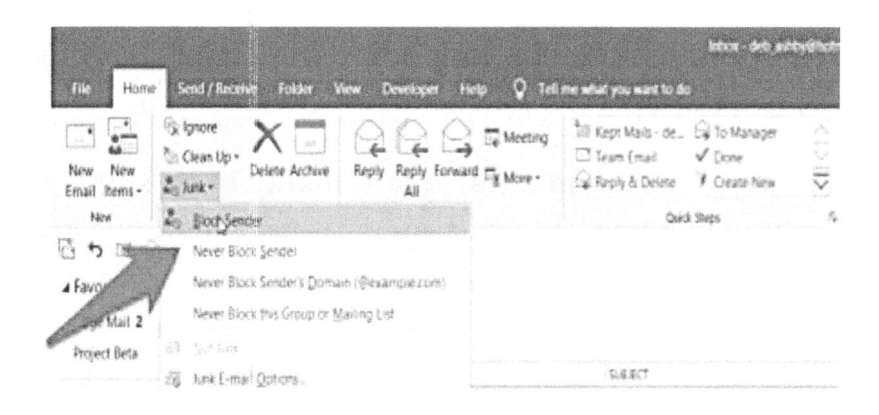

Choose the option you prefer from the following options:

No automatic filtering With this setting, every sleazy message will get straight into your inbox.

Low: Only the junkiest of junk will be moved, though some nasty mail will make it to your inbox.

High: This option is so aggressive that it will sometimes move some legitimate mail. If you choose this setting, check the Junk Email Folder frequently to be sure that important messages do not get marked as junk by mistake.

Safelists only: This setting will remove all messages from your inbox except the ones from certain people or organizations that have been designated in the Safe Senders lists.

The checkboxes at the lower part of the Options tab also provide a range of other choices:

Instead of moving it to the junk email folder, permanently delete the suspected junk email: This option might be a little too aggressive. There is just no perfect junk email filter yet. It might be better to drag junk messages to the junk email folder and manually empty the folder after it has been properly checked. If, however, you work with an organization that limits the amount of email you should store, this option might be just perfect for you.

Disable links and other functionality in phishing messages: The term "phishing" is used for an email message that attempts to impersonate a business or a financial institution in a bid to steal your personal information or have your laptop infected with a virus. This is most of the time the first step when it comes to operations of identity theft. As such, Outlook will try to get false emails and also make the web links ineffective. On no occasion should you release your personal information to any financial institution over the phone, It is best you do so over the phone or directly log on to its website.

Warn Me About Suspicious Domain Names in Email Addresses: There are some locations that have bad reputations both on and off the internet. If you get an email from a location that is suspicious, Outlook can give you a warning so you don't get into trouble.

- Click **on the OK button** and the Junk email dialog box will close.

Filtering your email with sender and recipient lists

The junk email feature in Outlook helps you make decisions if you would prefer to set up a safe and blocked list of your own. There is an option to make a list of people whose messages should be moved to this folder all the time. Take a look at the tabs of the Junk Email Options dialog box for a description of the specific types of senders that can be entered.

Whenever you receive a message from an email address or domain that is specified in this option, Outlook ensures it does not treat the message as a junk email, irrespective of the content of the message.

If you get a message from a mailing list online, the message might come from many different people, but it is always addressed to the list. In this case, the name of the list should always be on your safe recipient's list.

Blocked Senders: This is the direct opposite of the other choices above. Messages from the addresses or domains in this list are expected to always be treated as junk emails.

International: There are a lot of spam messages that come from abroad. There are times when you receive a long and endless list of spam from senders whose email addresses end up in strange letters like herte@spam.ru. The odd letters at the very end of the address are known as top-level domains, and they also show the country of origin of the sender. For example,.ru is Russia's top-level domain, which is a common source of spam these days.

Furthermore, if you receive lots of spam messages in foreign languages, you can also set Outlook to ban messages like that. Locate the international tab, select the Blocked Encoding List icon, and choose the various languages.

If you also receive legitimate emails regularly from senders whose messages make use of a particular top-level domain, and you don't want to block that domain even if you receive a lot of spam from it, Do not block the languages that are used by these legitimate senders.

To add a person to your Blocked Senders list, follow these steps:

- When you receive a message from someone you don't wish to hear from anymore, choose the message.

- Select **the Junk button located on the Home tab of the Ribbon**.

- Select **the Block Sender option**.

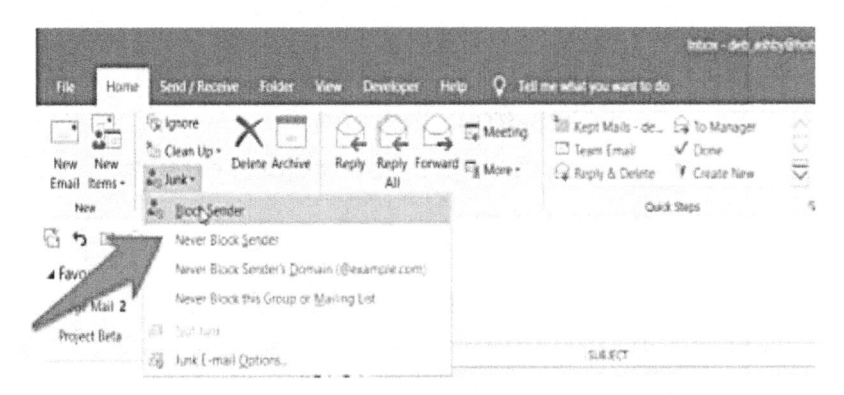

This method also works for adding people, domains, or groups to the Safe Recipients and Safe Senders lists. To be more precise, there is an option to go directly to the appropriate tab located in the Junk Email Options dialog box and insert the addresses or domains you prefer to sieve.

You could also save time by using the following junk email options:

- At the bottom of the Safe Senders tab is the option labeled "Also Trust Email From My Contacts." By checking this box, all messages from anyone in your address book will be treated as safe.

- **Recipients:** In Outlook, if you check the box labeled "Automatically Add People I Email to the Safe Senders list," messages will be accepted from the people to whom you have already sent messages.

- **Import and Export:** Adding a long list of people to your Safe Senders or Blocked Senders list can be done in Notepad and then imported into Outlook. A company with a large client list may offer this option to all its employees.

Filtering domains

When it comes to junk mail choices in Outlook, you have one rather powerful option you should be aware of. The option has to do with sieving domains. By following these steps, you can enter the entire company in your Safe Senders list if you do business with someone at that company.

- Go **to the Mail module** > select **the message**.

- From the Home tab on the Ribbon, select **the Junk button**.

- Set the option to **Never Block the Sender's domain**

Archiving for Posterity

It doesn't take long for your message inbox to overwhelm you, faster than you can deal with it. Several people simply delete their messages after reading them. It is best to keep some messages for reference sake.

Storing too many messages slows Outlook down when you have a lot of them stored. Not only is a large collection of messages challenging to manage, in a large organization you may not be allowed to store many emails to prevent them from clogging up the server.

Outlook has an archive feature that you can use to store messages and other items that you no longer need to view but that may be useful in the future. By reducing the number of emails you store in the email system, you can easily get along with your system administrators if you use Outlook on an Exchange network at work. You may see that your Outlook items are disappearing if you use the AutoArchive feature to automatically archive items.

Below you will find instructions on finding items that Outlook has archived for you to keep. People tend to archive email messages most often, but nearly all Outlook items can be archived, including calendars and tasks.

Setting up Auto Archive

The AutoArchive setting of Outlook prevents Outlook from automatically archiving your items unless you change it. However, some businesses may allow their users to use it.

You should check your company's email retention policy before you make any changes to the AutoArchive settings. Some companies use an auto-delete service to delete old messages.

Follow these steps if you want to enable AutoArchive, see how Outlook archives items, or change how Outlook works:

- Click **the File tab** and choose **Options**. The Outlook Options dialog box will then be opened.

- In the navigation pane on the left, click **the "Advanced" button**.

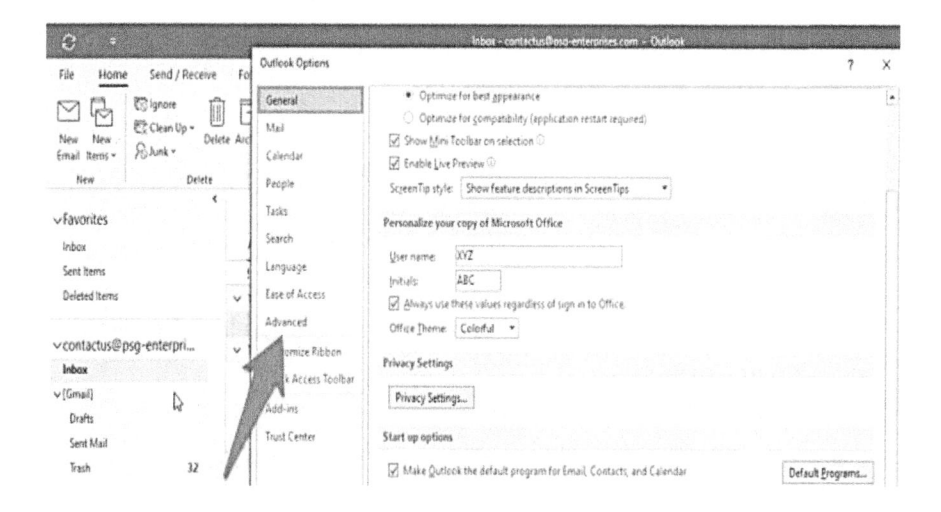

- A menu of options appears for working with Outlook pages.

- Go to the AutoArchive section and click **the AutoArchive Settings button**.

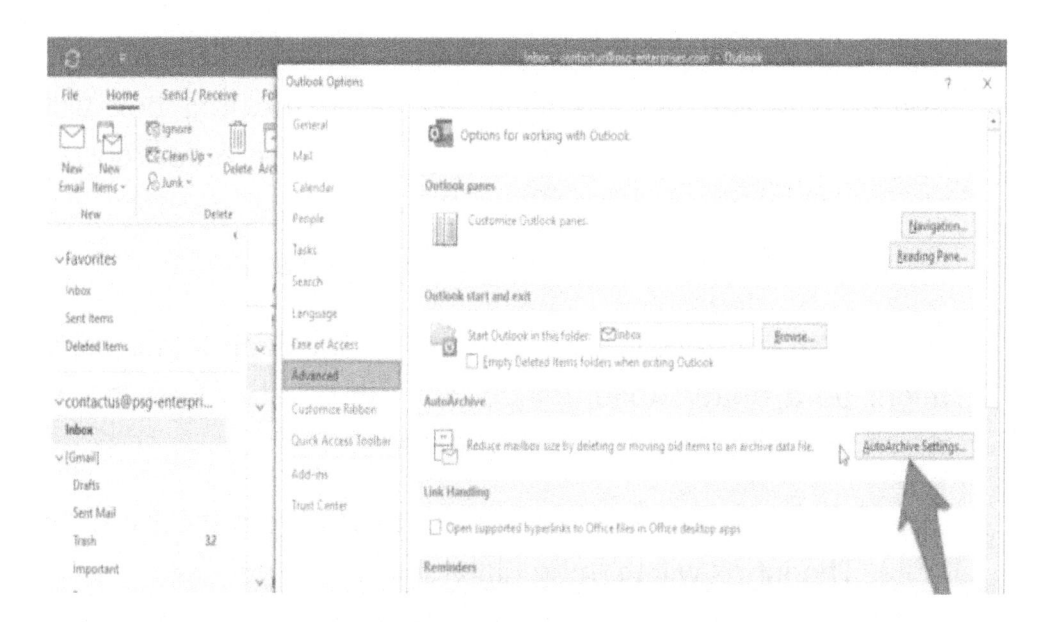

It's best to avoid making radical changes to the AutoArchive dialog box, at least not until you look at what's already set up.

A couple of important tidbits that are normally provided by the AutoArchive dialog box are:

- Is the Auto Archive feature enabled or not?

- What is the frequency at which Outlook archives items?

- How old do items have to be in order to be archived by Outlook?

- Identify the location and name of the archive.

AutoArchive turns on automatically every 14 days without changing any of the other AutoArchive settings, sending items older than 6 months to the archive file shown in the AutoArchive dialog box.

At the top of the Auto Archive dialog box, you can select or deselect the "Run AutoArchive Every" check box to turn on or off the AutoArchive process. Replace the 14 in the text box with any number between 1 and 60 to change how often AutoArchive runs.

Setting AutoArchive for individual folders

Having the AutoArchive settings set up for each folder separately might be a better option since you will be able to select exactly which files will be archived and which won't.

- From the Mail module, select **Inbox** from the list of folders. The inbox will then be highlighted.

- In the Properties group of the Ribbon, click the **AutoArchive Settings button** under the Folder tab.

- A dialog box with **Inbox Properties appears**, showing the **AutoArchive tab.**

- Using these settings, archive **the selected folder**.

- Make sure the drop-down menu is set to Months.

- Messages that are very recent from your inbox can be auto-archived if you choose "Weeks."

- Clean Out Items Older Than Type 6 if it doesn't already appear in the Clean Out Items Older Than text box.

- You should now see a notification that items older than six months will be deleted.

- It is possible to auto archive messages from the inbox that are anywhere between one day old and 999 months old by entering any number between 1 and 999.

- Choose to **Move Old Items to the Default Archive Folder**.

- It is likely that this setting is already selected, but make sure the option to permanently delete old items is not selected.

- Choosing this option would remove all old inbox messages instead of archiving them.

- To proceed, click **the OK button.**

- Even though you're only setting the AutoArchive settings for a single folder, you must enable Outlook's AutoArchive option.

To use AutoArchive with each folder, repeat these steps. You should at least check what the current AutoArchive settings are for any folder you do not want to auto-archive.

By enabling Outlook's AutoArchive feature, you probably enabled AutoArchive for some other folders that you might not want to archive; there is no way to auto archive a folder without also turning on Outlook's AutoArchive setting.

Whenever you create a new folder, it's automatically set not to auto-archive, even if you previously applied your auto-archiving settings for all folders. If you want your new folder to autoarchive, go through the previous steps for that folder. Also, when you turn on Auto Archive for Outlook, the Deleted Items folder is set to auto archive using the default settings. If you don't clean out your Deleted Items folder, all the emails you thought you'd never see again will instead be archived for posterity. You should consider setting the Deleted Items folder to not auto-archive.

Starting the archive process manually

Here are the steps you can follow to archive messages at any time:

- Navigate **to the File tab**.
- In the left-hand navigation pane, click **the Info button**.
- Go to **Tools and click on it**.
- The Archive dialog box appears when you click **"Clean Up Old Items."**
- Then click **OK** once you've selected your settings.

Manually starting an archive will give you a better sense of control over the process and enable you to:

- Establish a deadline for archiving items (say, the first of the year).

- Archive the appropriate folders and place the items in the archive.

- Create different archive files for different Outlook folders.

One disadvantage of all these controls is that it's possible to accidentally archive something and not be able to find it again.

If you want to keep track of your archived items, don't change the name or location of the files to which your archived items are sent. Outlook doesn't provide much assistance here.

Finding and viewing archived items

AutoArchive can sometimes seem like magic. Objects from the past are mysteriously filed away without any action from you.

It seems simple enough, doesn't it? You may not notice it, but when you suddenly need one of those items that appeared in your archive, you will. Then you have to figure out where it went and how it got there.

Using these steps, you can open a data file containing archive items:

- Navigate to **the File tab**, click on **Open & Export**, then select **Open Outlook Data File**. A dialog box for opening Outlook data files appears.

- Choose **the file** you wish to open. The filename of the selected file appears in the File Name text box. For example, to open the default archive file, select **"archive."**

- Click on **the OK button**. In the Navigation pane, below your normal set of folders, you can see the name of the data file you opened.

The following steps will help you determine the name of the archived data file to open:

- Navigate **to the File tab**.

- Click on **"Info"**.

- Select **the Tools button**.

- Click on **the "Clean Up Old Items" button.**

- Look in the text box for the Archive File.

- The archive file is located here. Please do not change the information; otherwise, Outlook might start sending your archived items to another location.

In the Archive File text box, you will usually find a lot of complex information with colons and slashes and other things that everyone can't understand.

Closing the archive data file

Archive data files can remain open in the Folder pane for as long as you like, although most people close them once they locate what they're looking for.

You can speed up Outlook by closing unnecessary data files.

Follow these steps to close an archived data file:

- Right-click on **the archive data file's name** in the Folder pane. An options menu appears.

- The Archive can be closed by selecting "Close." If the archive data file is called something else than an archive, the name of the archive data file will replace the term "archive."

In the folder pane, your archive folder disappears.

Arranging Your Messages

There is no one who gets a little email anymore. When you get one message, you get a lot of them, which quickly fills up your inbox. The next thing you know, you're scrolling through a never-ending stream of messages, trying to find the one needle in the haystack that you needed a week ago.

Thanks to Outlook, you have a bunch of options for organizing your inbox so you can figure out what is important, what can wait, and what can be ignored.

Whenever Outlook displays the reading pane on the right side of the screen, four labels appear at the top of the list of messages.

Two of the leftmost labels are titled "All" and "Unread." When you click on any of your messages, they are all displayed. Messages you haven't read yet will appear if you click Unread; once you read a message, it will disappear from this view, although you can see it again if you click All.

On the right, you can see the system Outlook uses to organize the order in which your messages are displayed. Your messages are displayed in chronological order if the "By Date" label is displayed. Most of the time, you'll want to see your messages that way.

Below are other ways in which messages can be arranged:

Date of Conversations:

Your inbox will look like this when you first set up Outlook. Messages are displayed in the order of receipt, just as you would expect.

From:

The arrangement, as you might guess, organizes your message collection according to the person who sent the message.

While setting up a search folder can sometimes be faster than using the From arrangement, a search folder can still be the best way to track messages from specific people.

In order to:

Not all the messages you receive are addressed to you. In some cases, you receive messages addressed to a list of people, so you don't see your name in the To field. The To field of each message is separated according to whether your name appears in it.

Categories:

In either case, messages can be sorted based on categories if you choose to use them. For IMAP accounts, this option may not be available.

Flag:

If you have flagged items with a due date, it is helpful to sort messages by start date or due date. When sorting in ascending order, flagged items appear last, and when sorting in descending order, they appear first.

Just like Categories, the option might not be available for an IMAP account.

Dimensions:

Certain system administrators care about size, and it isn't always a personal issue. Your company's email servers can get clogged up with images, music, and other heavyweight files that are attached to email messages.

If your system administrator asks you to thin out your inbox, take advantage of this feature: Identify overweight messages and delete or archive them.

Microsoft Outlook categorizes messages as "Tiny," "Small, "Medium, "Huge, or "Enormous," and perhaps it will add "Ginormous" in its next version.

Subject:

While this arrangement is similar to conversations, it doesn't follow the thread of a conversation; it merely groups together messages with the same subject matter. Messages with the same subject do not necessarily belong to the same conversation.

Type:

The items that arrive in your inbox are not always simple messages; you can also receive meeting requests, task requests, etc.

Use the type arrangement so the most interesting messages rise to the top of the list when you want to separate messages from meeting requests and so on.

Attachments:

You may not be looking for a message when you go to your inbox; you may be looking for an attachment. When you arrange your messages by attachment, you have the chance to look for the likely targets first.

Account:

Outlook can collect emails from several different email addresses simultaneously, and each email address gets its own inbox.

Having said that, if you move messages from different email addresses into the same folder, as you might do when you clean up your inbox periodically, at some point you may want to know which messages came from which address or just want to see those messages sent from that address. Click **the arrow** next to the name of any account you do not want to see if you want to see only the messages sent to that address.

As a result, Outlook only displays messages from accounts that you are interested in. As long as all your incoming mail is consolidated into a single inbox, the account arrangement won't be useful when

Importance: If you need to see high-priority messages first, this is the arrangement to choose.

While the reading pane is off, use the following instructions to arrange your messages:

On the View tab, select the arrangement you want to use from the Arrangement group, and then click **Reverse Sort** to reverse the order of sorts.

Viewing conversations

No matter if you simply exchange a few emails back and forth with one person or take part in a large group discussion that lasts for weeks, Outlook's Conversations arrangement keeps all related messages on the same subject grouped together.

At a glance, you can view the most recent message in a conversation thread as well as older messages from the conversation at a glance.

Whenever someone replies to a message, either by **clicking Reply or Reply All,** a conversation begins. All new messages become part of the conversation regardless of who else responds or contributes.

You can enable conversation viewing by following these steps.

- Click **the View tab** in the Mail module.
- In the Messages group, select **the "Show as Conversations" check box**.

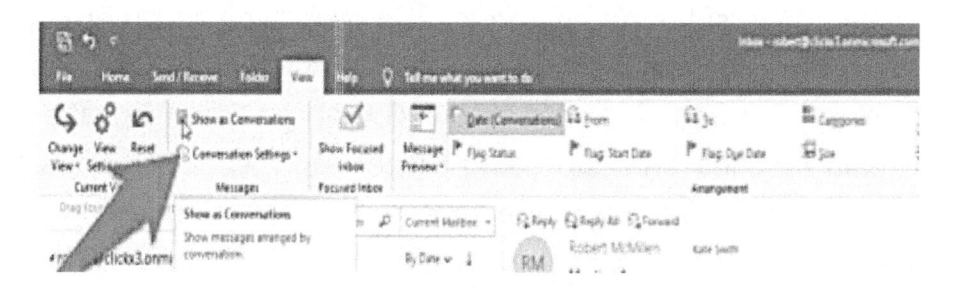

In your inbox, a small triangle just to the left of the sender's name indicates that more messages are included in the conversation if the conversation display is enabled.

The most recent message that was received in the conversation appears in the Reading pane when you click on a message that's part of a conversation. To view all the messages you have sent or received as part of the conversation, click the triangle to the left of the message's mail icon.

It is possible for some of these messages to appear in the conversation list even if they are in the Sent folder or have been moved to another folder. Messages that are moved to the Deleted Items folder, however, will not appear in the conversation list.

All messages in a conversation can be replied to. Replying to a message that isn't the latest displays a warning and gives you the option of opening the latest message.

If you want to customize the display of conversations,

- Click **the Conversation Settings button on the Ribbon**. It will bring up a menu of options. For instance, you may choose to show or hide messages from other folders.

Ignoring conversations

The conversation often comes to a point where you are no longer interested or relevant to the discussion. Off-topic discussions are not uncommon. A simple discussion about when to have the next team meeting ends up being a seemingly endless series of jokes about how hot it gets in the conference room during the winter.

Whenever you no longer wish to follow a conversation, you can easily ignore it:

On the Home tab, click **the Ignore button** next to the appropriate message.

To ignore a conversation, right-click **on any message** and select **Ignore** from the menu; or **select any message and press Ctrl+Delete**.

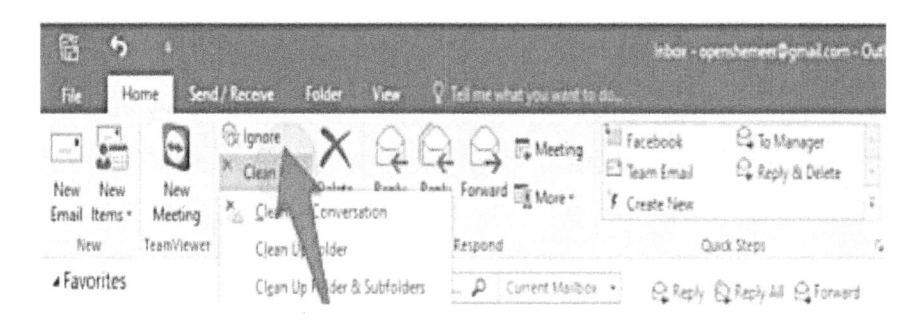

As soon as you ignore a conversation, all messages from that conversation, whether in your inbox or in any other folder, will be moved to the Deleted Items folder.

The messages from the conversation that is in your Sent folder are not moved. Your inbox and other folders are free of traces of the conversation.

Additionally, any new messages from the conversation are automatically sent to the Deleted Items folder.

Cleaning up conversations

Most email programs automatically include the text of the original message in the reply when someone replies to a message. Upon the first installation of Outlook, it does this by default.

You can see this setting by:

- Navigating to **the File tab** > Select **the Options button** in the left-hand Navigation pane

- In the Outlook Options dialog box, click **the Mail tab**, then scroll down to the Replies and Forwards section.

As long as everyone replies to a conversation with the text of the previous message, each subsequent message becomes a snapshot of the entire conversation thread up to that point.

As a result, there is a lot of redundancy in the messages because the same information is repeated. Is that needed? Messages that contain information already included in another message can be removed from a conversation if Outlook detects this redundancy. The process is known as "cleaning up" in Outlook.

If you want to clean up a conversation quickly,

Select **the message** you want to delete > **press Alt+Delete**.

To clean up more thoroughly, follow these steps:

- Select **the conversation** you want to clean up in the Mail module.
You'll see the message that was most recently received in the conversation. Any folder containing a message from the conversation can be used to do this.

- Click **the Clean Up button** in the Delete group on the Home tab of the Ribbon.
A drop-down box appears with three options.

-

- Select **Clean Up Conversation**.

    When Outlook detects that the messages in a conversation are redundant, it removes them from all the folders they're in and moves them to the Deleted Items folder. However, messages in the "sent" folder remain in the folder. As another option, you can select **"Clean Up Folder"** to clear out all conversations within the selected folder. It goes a step further by cleaning up all the conversations in the selected folders as well as all subfolders.

As an example, if you have a personal folder inside your inbox folder, selecting the inbox folder and then choosing Clean Up Folder & Subfolder will automatically clear out all conversations in both folders.

Outlook won't remove many messages by itself, so don't be surprised. Outlook takes a conservative approach when it comes to eliminating redundant messages, and it also doesn't move replies that modify a previous message or that are marked as a follow-up.

The following settings will allow Outlook more flexibility in what it can move when cleaning up a conversation:

- Click **on the File tab and then Options.** A dialog box with Outlook options opens.

- Select **the "Mail" button**. A window opens with the mail settings.

- The conversation cleanup section can be found at the bottom.
  Outlook offers several options that control when it moves

messages from conversations and when it does not. Choose the settings that work for you.

Make sure you pay attention to the Cleaned-Up Items Will Go to This Folder text box. Cleaning up items in Outlook places them in the Deleted Items folder by default. However, if you wish to send cleaned-up items elsewhere, such as a folder in an archive file, this is the place where you make the change. Select a destination location from the Browse button.

Simplifying Tasks Using Quick-Steps

It is no doubt any longer a secret that Outlook actions can require multiple clicks of the mouse to complete, like replying to a message and then deleting it. When you perform a particular action in Outlook only occasionally, it's not a big deal, but if you do it regularly, it can quickly get tedious.

Outlook Quick-Steps can come in handy if you perform certain tasks on a regular basis. Multi-step tasks can be reduced to a single click with Quick-Steps.

On the Ribbon's Home tab, under the Mail module, you can find Quick-Steps. Despite Quick-Steps only appearing when you are working with the mail module, this tool can help you speed up most actions in Outlook, such as those involving the calendar and tasks.

Move To:

If you often move messages into a specific folder, use this Quick-Step. The Quick-Step displays Move To: If you have yet to move a message to a folder in Outlook, This Quick-Step replaces the To which folder you moved the message to, such as "Move To: Personal." If you have already moved messages to folders,

To the supervisor:

In this Quick-Step, the selection of a message is automatically forwarded to a particular recipient, but the message is not deleted. Generally, if you are using Outlook in a corporate setting, the message you are reading is forwarded to your manager.

Team Email:

By using this Quick-Step, you are able to open the New Message form and fill in the To field with a specific group of recipients. It's usually set up in a corporate environment by your administrators to open a message already addressed to all members of your team, including your manager and everyone directly reporting to your manager. There's no need to limit your emails to your boss and your colleagues; you can include whomever you choose in a group. Groups are created in the People module.

Delete & Reply:

When this Quick-Step is selected, Outlook automatically opens a message form for replying to the sender and moves the selected message to the Deleted Items folder.

Create A New:

The Edit Quick-Step Wizard, which can be customized to suit your own needs, is technically not a Quick-Step; it merely opens the Edit Quick-Step Wizard.

Every Quick-Step, except reply and delete, requires you to make a decision the first time you use it. This is because Outlook doesn't know yet who your manager is, where your messages should be moved to, etc. As a result, you'll have to tell Outlook what to do when you select a specific Quick-Step. Once you've done this,

Outlook will remember what you want it to do whenever you select the Quick-Step.

Here are the Quick-Steps as an example, but each is a bit different:

- Select **an inbox message from the Mail module**. Any message will do. Move the message without worrying about its actual location. If you're using Move To Quick-Step for the first time, Outlook will not move the message you select; it only needs to know the type of Outlook element you're creating the Quick-Step for.

- The icon in the upper-left corner of the Quick-Steps box appears when you click the Home tab. There might be **a "Move To:" text underneath the icon**. A dialog box appears for the first time. You might not see **"Move To:"** Instead, you might see a folder name, such as Personal. If the First Time Setup dialog box has already been pre-populated with a folder name, Outlook is just helpfully suggesting the last folder you moved a message to; the dialog box will still appear.

- Choose **where Quick-Step will move the messages**. The Move to Folder box will appear. Click **the arrow near the end of the box** to select a folder. **You can also select "Other Folder"** if you don't see the folder you want. This will open a window displaying all the folders available. The **"Select Folder"** option even allows you to create new folders.

- Ensure that the Move to Folder check box is selected. Mark as Read must also be selected if you want each message to be marked as read as soon as the Quick-Step moves it.

In order to access Quick-Step's settings, click **the Options button**. From there you can change the icon, add actions, and create keyboard shortcuts.

- Fill out the Name text box with the name of your Quick-Step. The moment you clicked the Move to Folder box, Outlook also added the folder's name to the Name text box. Skip ahead to Step 2 if you like the name Outlook chose for the Quick-Step. Simply type a different name into the Name text box if you want to name the Quick-Step something else. The Quick-Step should have a name that will make it easy for you to remember what it does. Do you agree that the "Move to Personal Folder" is an appropriate name for a Quick-Step that moves a message to a folder called Personal? Personal also works for those with a preference for brevity.

- To save, **click the Save button.**
  This closes the First Time Setup dialog box.

Creating and managing Quick-Steps

Outlook includes a number of Quick-Step templates in addition to the ones shown in the Quick-Step box upon installation. To access these additional Quick-Step templates, **follow these steps:**

- Click on **the Home tab** and locate **the Quick-Step box's scroll bar** (located on the right side of the Quick-Step box; it has one up and two down arrows). Click the arrow at the bottom (the one with a line above it).

  Upon hovering over "New Quick-Step", two options appear at the bottom: Manage Quick-Steps and New Quick-Step.

- Select **Create New Quick-Step**.

  You will see more Quick-Step templates. Any of these templates open the First Time Setup dialog box, which offers choices based on the type of task you selected. If, for instance, you select Move to Folder, the First Time Setup dialog box asks where the messages will be moved, as well as whether you want to mark them as read. Other Quick-Step templates include:

  - **Move to Folder:** Simply put, this is the same as "Move To."

  - **Categorize & Move:** The selected message is moved to a specific folder, marked as read, and assigned a color and name for the category. You might not see this if you're using an IMAP account.

  - **Flag & Move:** The selected message will be moved to the appropriate folder, marked as read, and given a flag.

  - **New Email To:** Here you can open a form already filled out with a particular recipient's name in the To field.

  - **To:** Essentially the same as Manager.

- **New Meeting:** In cases where you frequently invite the same people to meetings, this Quick-Step will automatically fill in the To field with the invitees.

- **Custom: Clicking this will open the** Edit Quick-Step dialog box, which allows you to customize your own Quick-Step.

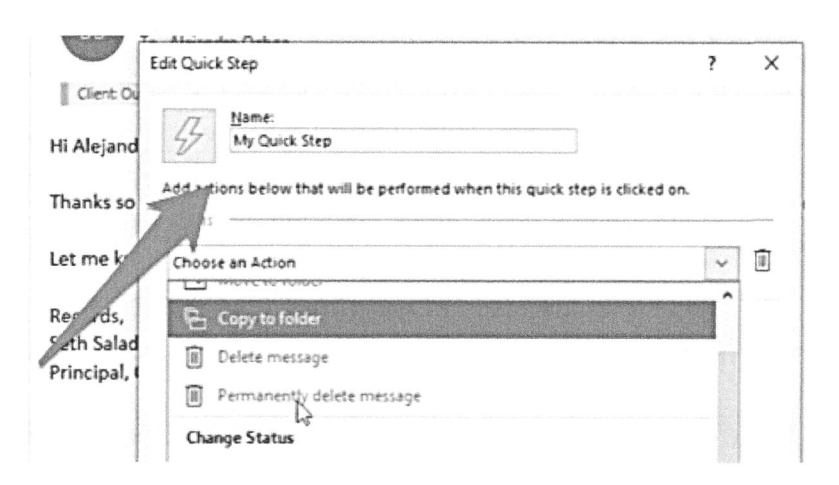

- Choose **a template** from the Quick-Step menu. A First Time Setup dialog box opens as you see when you click Move To Quick-Step.

- Decide on a template name and make your selections. Depending on the task, you'll have to instruct Outlook where a message should go, how to categorize a message, what flags to set, who to send or forward a message to, or whom to invite to a meeting. Be sure to also name this Quick-Step so that you will remember what it does when you input this information into the First Time Setup dialog box.

- Click on **the Finish button**.
  You will see the First Time Setup dialog box close.

Creating Quick Parts to save keystrokes

Frequently used text can be saved as a Quick Part to help you save time and effort when typing it into email messages over and over. It's not the same thing as Quick-Steps, but they're ridiculously simple.

The steps for creating a quick part are as follows:

- You can open a reply message in a new window after clicking **"Pop Out"** while composing it in the Reading pane. This is because you need to access the Insert tab, and you don't get this when composing or replying in the Reading pane.

- The text in the message can be selected by dragging your mouse over it. The selected text will be highlighted.

- In the Text group on the Ribbon, click **the Insert tab** >select **Quick Parts**. An option will appear.

- Select **"Save Selection to Quick Part Gallery."** The dialog box for creating building blocks appears.

- If you don't like the name of your quick part, type a new one. You may like the current name, but you might want to change it. A Quick Part can also be assigned a category and a description, but these options don't make much difference in how you use it, so you can leave them out.

- To proceed, click **OK**.

You can quickly add a Quick Part to the body of a new email or reply by clicking the **Insert tab** on the Ribbon, followed by Quick Parts in the Text group, and then **clicking the Quick Part** you want. Once you try it, you won't want to send an original email again.

CHAPTER 7

MANAGING CONTACTS, DATES, TASKS AND MORE

Learn how to create and manage your Contacts list, including changing how you view your contacts, attaching photos to them, and sending them to other people, as well as how to sort your contacts and use grouped views.

Discover how to create and modify appointments, print your calendar, and work with multiple calendars using the Calendar.

In addition to allowing you to keep your entire list of names and addresses in one place, Outlook also lets you sort, view, find, and print it in many different ways, depending on the type of work you're doing. Furthermore, you can store lists of family and friends alongside your business contacts in Outlook, so you can easily distinguish between them when necessary.

Putting in Your Contacts' Names, Numbers, and Other Stuff

Keeping a large number of names, numbers, and addresses is not difficult, but finding them again in the future requires magic unless you have an application like Outlook. Several programs can save names and related numbers, but Outlook is the most popular choice for working with names, addresses, and phone numbers.

You'll be familiar with the Outlook Contacts feature if you've ever used a pocket address book. You just need to enter the name, address, phone number, and a few tidbits-and you're done!

The quick and dirty way to enter contacts.

A new contact can be added easily to your Contacts list:

- To create a new contact, click **the New Contact button** in the People module. A contact form will appear.

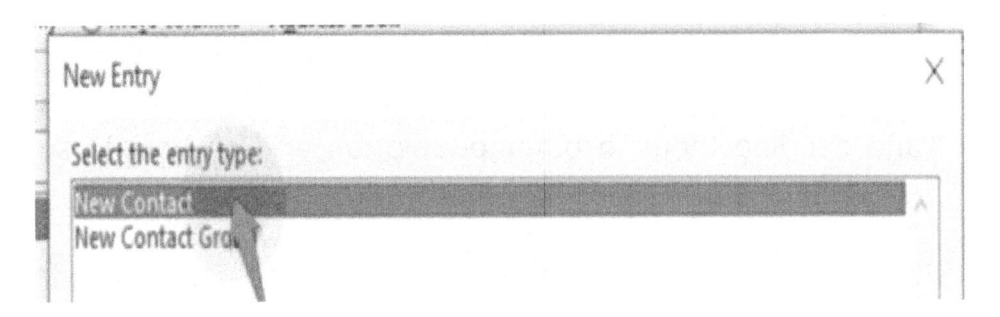

- Complete the form. It is not necessary to fill out all the fields; only use those that pertain to the contact in question.

- Close the document by clicking **Save & Close**. It's really that simple. Adding more information to contact later is okay if you don't fill in all the details immediately.

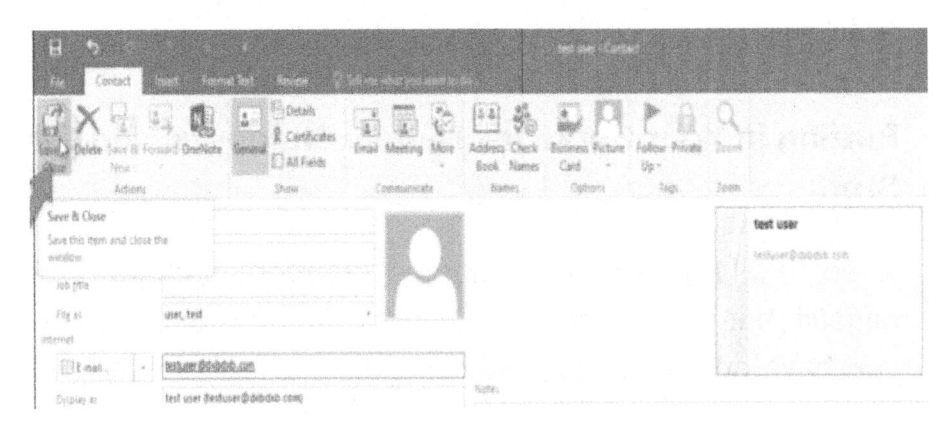

The slow, complete way to enter contact

Depending on your preferences, you can enter literally dozens of details about every person on your contacts list. However, if you just want to include the essentials, that's fine. Here's what you'll need to do to enter every tiny detail for every contact record.

Select "New Contact" from the People module.

You will see the new contact form.

- Choose **your full name** from the drop-down menu. A window titled "Check Full Name" appears.

- **Take one or more of the following actions:**

    ○ To scroll down, click **the triangle** (called the "scroll-down button") on the right edge of the text box named "Title." You can either **type a title** (such as Reverend, Guru, or Swami) or select **one from the drop-down menu**.

    ○ Enter **the contact's first name** in the first text box.

    ○ If necessary, type **the contact's middle initial** (if any). Leave this field blank if there is no middle initial. The middle name can also be written here if you wish.

    ○ Enter **the contact's last name** in the "Last" text box.

    ○ Select **the suffix from the drop-down menu**. Select one of the options (like Jr., III, or Ph.D.), or type one in the box (such as D.D.S., B.P.O.E.).

- To proceed, click **the OK button**.

    Your Full Name and File NumberAs text boxes are now filled with the name you entered in the Check Full Name dialog box,

- Complete the form by **clicking on the appropriate box** and entering **the requested information.**
Please leave the box blank if the information is unavailable, for example, if a contact does not have a title. There are more options when a triangle appears after the box. If your choice isn't listed, enter it in the box.

    ○ When you enter a name in the Full Name box, you'll see that name appear in the File As box.

    ○ You can file a person under a different name by clicking **File As** and entering the designation you prefer. Your dentist may, for example, be filed under the term "dentist" rather than by name. In the alphabetical listing, the dentist's name appears under "dentist" rather than under the actual name. In your contacts list, you will find the full name and the file as designations. By doing so, you can find your dentist either by name or by the word "dentist."

- Enter **the email address** of your contact in the "Email" text box.
To enter a second email address, click **Email 2**, pick the second address from the list, and then enter it in the text box.

- Type **the business phone number** of the contact in the text box beside "Business Phone."

- You will have the option to type in the contact's home phone number if you click on the Home Phone text box. In order to enter numbers other than home and business telephones, click **the triangle beside the number option**, choose **the type of number** you are entering, and then **enter the number.**

There are four blocks for phone numbers in the New Contact form. The drop-down menu contains 19 different types of phone numbers that you can use according to the types of numbers your contacts have.

- Choose **the type of address** you want to enter in the Addresses section by **clicking the triangle**.
  Choose **either a business address, a home address, or some other address.**

- Go to the Addresses section and click **the button**.
  An address check dialog box appears.

- **Fill in the appropriate fields with the following information:**

    - The street

    - The city, state,

    - The province

    - Region of zipping or postal code

    - Country

- Click **OK** to close the Check Address dialog box.

- If the address you just entered will be used for mailing, select the "This Is the Mailing Address" box on the New Contact form.

- If you want the address card to link directly to a page, click in the Web Page Address text box and type the page's address. A contact's webpage can be viewed by opening a contact record, clicking on the More button on the Ribbon, and

clicking Web Page (or pressing Ctrl+Shift+X). An internet browser will display the webpage.

The URL of the page can be viewed in your web browser by entering it into the Address box. Within the Web Page Address text box, you can enter the URL for any webpage an Outlook contact has.

Fill in the bottom right notes box with whatever information you want.

There is no limit to what you can enter (preferably something that will help in your dealings with the contact).

- Click **the Save & Close button** on the Ribbon after you are finished.
When you've entered any information you need (or may need) to know about the people you deal with at work, you're ready to start interacting.

Viewing the contacts

The information you enter in Outlook can be viewed in many different and useful ways, called views. By viewing your contact information and sorting the views, you can easily see the big picture of the data you've entered. Within each module, Outlook provides several predefined views. You can edit any predefined view, name it, save it, and then use it exactly as you would the predefined views.

You can change how your contacts list appears by following these steps:

- Select **the Home tab from the Ribbon** of the People module.

- Choose **the view you want from the Current View group**. That view will appear on the display. Besides the card view, you can also select the phone view, the list view, or any other view you like.

View Sorting

A few views, such as the phone view of the People module, are organized as simple lists.

You can sort by a column's title once you've clicked on its title if you can't find a contact in a view with columns. Suppose you want to know the names of the IBM employees in your contacts list. If you sort the company column, you can see all the names at the same time.

Here are the steps you need to follow to sort by column name:

- Select **the Phone view** on the Ribbon under the Current View section of the People module.
  Contacts are displayed in the phone view.

- Go **to the COMPANY column** and click **the heading**. Contacts are listed alphabetically from A to Z (or ascending order) according to the "company" column. Now you can find someone by scrolling to that letter. By sorting by company, all contacts appear in alphabetical order of company name.

Upon clicking the title a second time, you will see your contacts sorted in reverse alphabetical order (i.e., descending order).

Rearranging Views

Simply drag the title of a column and drop it where you want it to appear to rearrange the appearance of a view. Below is an example of how to move

You can display the contacts list in the Phone view by clicking **the Phone button** in the Current View group on the Home tab.

The contacts list may already be displayed in the phone view.

- To the left of the FILE AS column, click on **the title** of the preferred column and drag it over.
  Red arrows appear to the left of the clicked column, pointing to the border between two columns. By releasing the mouse button, Outlook will drop the column where the red arrows indicate.

- Let go of the mouse button. You have now dragged the column from the right to the left. The procedure is the same for moving any column in Outlook.

Using grouped views

Sorting doesn't always suffice. After a while, you can easily accumulate several thousand contacts; it only takes a few years. In a long list, if you're looking for something with the letter M, for instance, you'll find it about three feet below the bottom of the screen, regardless of how you sort it.

There is no need for Outlook, Anonymous groups are the solution. You already have several predefined lists that rely on grouping in Outlook.

Lists are displayed in Outlook in several different ways: Sorted lists are like playing cards laid out in numerical order, starting with twos and proceeding to threes, fours, and so on, up to picture cards. In a group view, all the hearts, the spades, the diamonds, and then the clubs are arranged together in a single row.

Here are the steps to viewing the company grouping in list view:

- Select **the Home tab** under the People module.

- Select **the List option** from the Current View group **on the Home tab**.
  Companies are represented by headings with the prefix "company". The number of items under each heading is shown under that heading.
  Expanding or collapsing the contacts under that heading is done by clicking **the triangle symbol** to the left of the heading.

You can group items according to just about anything you want, provided that the data you enter is accurate.

Below are the steps for grouping by another field:

- Select **View Settings** from the View tab of the People module.
  A dialog box with advanced view settings for the list appears. You will see that Group By is set to "company."

- group **by clicking "group by."**
  An appropriate dialog box opens. You will see that Group Items By is set to "Company."

- Select **a different field** from the company list.

- Specify the sort order by **clicking "Ascending" or "Declining."**
  Ascending means going from A to Z, and descending means going from Z to A.

- For the dialog box to close, **click OK**.

- Close the Advanced View Settings: List window by **clicking OK**.

Identifying Your Friends

A string tied around your finger doesn't do much to remind you to do something that involves another person, and it looks ridiculous as well. Fortunately, Outlook provides a better solution. You can easily remember the name of someone you have promised to call next week by flagging their name in the Contacts list. This will trigger a reminder in your calendar. Flagging isn't limited to contacts. The same effect can be achieved by adding reminders to tasks, emails, and appointments.

The following steps will guide you through the process of adding flags to contacts:

- You can flag a contact by **right-clicking** on it in the People module. You'll see a shortcut menu appear.

- Select **Follow Up. "**
  You will see the "Follow Up" menu. Choose **the day** for your follow-up.
  You have the option of choosing today, tomorrow, this week, or next week. When you flag a contact for a specific day, that contact's name appears in your Outlook Calendar on that day.

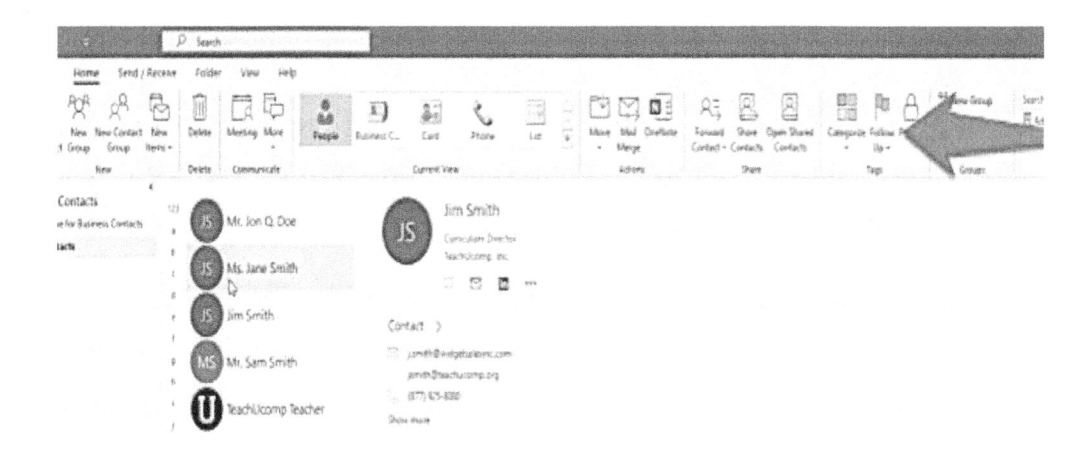

- Select **the contact,** click "**Follow Up,**" then add a reminder. A dialog box appears.
  If you need to avoid that person for some reason, you can choose to have the reminder open and a sound played at the time you specify. Reminders are Outlook's way of telling you to do something.

- The Custom dialog box allows you to select a reminder date from the Date drop-down menu in the Reminder section. A calendar is displayed when the arrow next to the date is clicked. Click on **the date** you want.

- From the drop-down menu, select **a time** for a reminder.

- Set the reminder **by clicking OK**.

Using Contact Information

I bet you intend to use all that contact information you entered. Let me show you a few ways to dig through your contacts list for valuable nuggets.

Searching for contacts

It's crucial to enter people's contact information so that you can find them again in the future. Otherwise, what's the point of this whole process?

It's easy to find names in the People module. The module allows you to get names by browsing or searching anywhere. Just use the scroll bar to rapidly move through the contacts. You can search for contacts by entering a name, email address, or any other relevant text in the Search Contacts field and selecting what you want from the results.

Here's how you can do it from card view, which you have not yet used in an official capacity. It is similar to the Business Cards view, except the cards vary in size depending on what information they contain and they are arranged in columns.

In Card view, you can search for a contact by the last name by using the following steps:

- Select **the Card view** on the Home tab of the Ribbon in the People module.
  You will see the card view.

- You can enter a contact's last name by **clicking on the white space** below any card.
  This displays the first instance of that name and highlights its card heading.

The company where a contact works may be a factor in your search for their name. Alternatively, you might want to include all the people on your list who live in a certain state or people who make you feel a certain way (now there's something to include in their records). A search tool would then direct you to a specific contact in such a case.

Here are the steps you need to follow to search for a contact using the search tool:

- Enter the desired text in the Search Contacts box of the People module, using your favorite view.
  In your Contacts list, you will find the search box just below the ribbon. Only contacts containing the information you typed appear in your contacts list. If you don't find any contacts matching your search, double-check that you spelled the search text correctly.

- In the search box, click **the X button** at the far right end to remove the search filter.

Conversely, if you have only a fragment of the name you're seeking, Outlook can find that fragment wherever it is. When you search for "Geo," you will find George Washington and any other Georges on your contacts list, including Boy George and George of the Jungle (assuming they are all close friends of yours and they are on your contacts list).

Finding a contact from any Outlook module

You'd like to search for a person, but you're currently using another module. That's fine. Any Outlook module can be searched using the Search People box on the Home tab on the Ribbon.

The steps are as follows:

- Find people by **clicking on the "Seek People" box.** You will find it on the far right of the Home tab of any Outlook module.

- Enter **the contact's name**.

- To open that contact's record in Outlook, **press Enter.** When you enter only a few letters of a name, Outlook lists names that contain those letters, so you can choose the contact you had in mind. With the word "Wash," you can search for George Washington, Sam Washburn, and any other people on your list that include "Wash."

- To view a contact record, **double-click its name.**

Sending a business card

Any Outlook user (or any other application that is capable of displaying digital business cards) is able to forward an electronic business card to another Outlook user. There's no better way to share any contact record in your list with someone else.

The most obvious thing you may want to send this way is your own contact information.

- Create your own contact record in the People module. This record should contain all the information you need to send to someone.

- To send information to a contact record, **click twice on the record**.
  Clicking twice opens the contact record.

- From the Ribbon, click **the Forward button** under the Contact tab.
  Three options are provided: as a business card, as an internet card (vCard), or as a contact in Outlook.

- Select **the format** that suits you best.
  If you're unsure, select "Business Card." Both Outlook and Internet cards can be sent using that program. A new message is generated containing the contact information.

- Enter **the recipient's address in the "To" text box.**
  You can also choose a name from your address book by **clicking the "To" button**.

- Press **Alt+S** (or click the Send button).
  A message and vCard will be sent to the recipient.

Double-clicking the icon representing the business card in the message will add the business card to your Contacts list. An additional contact record will be created. You can now add the new name along with all the information on the business card to your contacts list by clicking the Save and Close button.

Alternatively, your business card can be forwarded by clicking the contact record and then selecting the Forward button in the Ribbon. The process is shorter, but you can only forward it as a business card or as an Outlook contact.

Gathering people into groups

A contact group that contains more than one person can be created in your People module. It allows multiple recipients to receive the same message. Contact groups can also be categorized (just as you can with individual contacts), and you can send a contact group as a message attachment to make it available to other Outlook users.

Creating a Contact Group

The process of creating a contact group is simply a matter of naming your list and selecting from the names you've stored on your system. Email addresses are the only pieces of information that a contact group keeps track of—not phone numbers or mailing addresses.

The following steps will guide you through creating a contact group in your People module:

- Press **Ctrl+Shift+L** on the keyboard to activate the New Contact Group button (or click the People module's Home tab on the Ribbon).
  A contact group list will be displayed.

- **Fill out** the Name box with the name you wish to assign to the Contact group.
- Select the "**From Outlook Contacts" option under "Add Members."**
  In the Select Members: Contacts dialog box, you see the names of available members on the left and the Members box at the bottom.
  You can include the email addresses of people not in your contacts list or any of your other Outlook Address Books by **following these steps:**

    o Pick **a new email contact** (not from Outlook Contacts).

    o Enter **the name and email address** of the person you wish to add in the Add New Member dialog box.

    o You can now click **OK.**

    o Continue with the remaining steps.

- To add someone to your contact group, double-click their name.
  A box called "Members" appears at the bottom of the dialog box when you double-click on a name.
- If you've picked all the names you want, click **OK**.

That closes the Select Members: Contacts dialog box.

- Using the **Save & Close button** (or **pressing Alt + S**) will save and close your document.
  Your contact group will appear in your contacts list once the contact group dialog box has been closed.

Editing a contact group

Like everywhere else, people come and go in contact groups. Fortunately, you can edit the contacts:

- To view the names of your contact groups, **double-click** the group's name in the People module.
  An identical screen appears from when the group was created.

- **Use one or more of the following methods to edit the list:**

    - Remove a member from the list: Click **the name** and select "**Remove Member.**"

    - Select **a new member** from the names already in your contacts list: Click **on the Add Members** button and follow the same steps as when you created the list.

    - Add a person whose email address isn't listed in your contacts list: Select **the Add Members button**, click **on New Email Contact**, enter the person's name and email address, and then select **the OK button**.

- When you are finished editing the contact group, click **Save & Close**.

Adding pictures to contacts

A picture can be included with the contact information you gather- and not just for decoration. Due to the synchronization of many cell phones and other mobile devices with Outlook Contacts lists, you can view someone's picture when he or she calls or texts you. These pictures also appear when you view your Outlook contacts in Business Card view. When you forget names but never forget a face, you can save both names and faces.

You can add a picture to a contact record by following these steps:

- In the People module, **double-click** the contact whose picture will be displayed.
The contact's record will appear.

- **Click twice** on the picture icon in the center of the contact record.
A dialog box appears.

- **Double-click** the image you want to add to the location where it is located.
A picture of the contact will appear right in the contact's record.

- Save and close the document.

CHAPTER 8

UNLEASHING THE CALENDAR'S POWER

How long do people work during the day? Many people spend their days attending meetings. You can't stop meetings from happening, but the Outlook Calendar can simplify the scheduling process and help you schedule time for more meetings.

Getting Around the Outlook Calendar

Since you've been using calendars your whole life, you'll have no trouble understanding the Outlook Calendar. It looks like a calendar, with a row of dates for every day of the week plus weekends. You don't have to think like a computer to understand your schedule.

A mouse click on your calendar is usually all it takes to see more information about something. Click twice **if you need more details**. And if that is still not enough, there is a feature that can give you just what you need.

This feature actually goes by the name "Date Navigator," but don't confuse it with Casanova's chauffeur. It is a trick in Outlook that lets you change the part of the calendar you are viewing or the period of time you wish to see.

You can navigate through your calendar by following these steps:

- On the Navigation pane, click **on Calendar (or press Ctrl+2)**. The Information Viewer displays your calendar while the Date Navigator appears in the top part of the Navigation pane. The

Date Navigator also appears in the To-Do bar. Select **Day, Work Week, Week, or Month** from the drop-down menus. You will see the button you clicked highlighted.

- You can see the details of a single date by clicking **on it wherever it appears**. This displays the events and appointments scheduled for the day you clicked.

- The Date Navigator can be advanced one month at a time by clicking **the triangles next to the month name**.

- With time (so to speak), you'll find the calendar view that suits you best. Most of the time, you can leave Outlook running in the background to keep access to the information you need.

You can find an open date quickly by following these steps:

- Hold down **the Ctrl and G keys**.
"G" is short for "go to." The "Go To Date" dialog box opens with a selected date.

- The Date box is currently set to January 15, 2019, but you can change it as you normally would by typing the date you want in the box as usual.
Typing something like "45 days ago" or "93 days from now" is a great way to change dates. Give it a try. You can change dates in simple English in Outlook. If you want to go to today's date, just click **the Today button on the Home tab on the Ribbon**.

Meetings Galore: Scheduling appointments

Datebooks are vital to many people. Many people still use paper datebooks. I admit I like these datebooks best for putting stuff in them. However, once it's in, it's hard to find. Electronic gadgets like iPhones, Androids, and BlackBerrys (yes, there are still BlackBerrys!) can also act as datebooks, although sometimes it's hard to add appointments since they're small and don't use a mouse. With many digital gadgets synchronized with Outlook, you can have it all!

With Outlook, adding appointments is surprisingly easy-and finding items you've entered is even easier. You are also alerted when you schedule two appointments at once.

The quick and dirty way to enter an appointment

There are some appointments that don't require much explanation. No need to be a showoff about your appointment with Mom on Friday:

1. Make sure the view showing the hours of the day is selected in the Calendar module.
   Examples include a day, a week, and a workweek.

2. To view the appointment time on the desired day, click **the text box**.

3. Describe the appointment in detail.
   Mom's lunch, for example.

4. Click **the Enter key.**
   In no time at all, you will have your official appointment added to your schedule.

The complete way to enter an appointment

For lunch dates with Mom, you wouldn't need as much information as you would for your work appointments.

You may want to include:

- Meeting location details

- Agenda Notes for the meeting

- You can show your boss how long you spend with your clients by creating a category.

The following method must be used for giving an appointment a full treatment:

- On the Ribbon, click **New Appointment in the Calendar module**.
  The appointment form will appear, or you can press **Ctrl+N for the screen** to let you add a new appointment to your calendar.

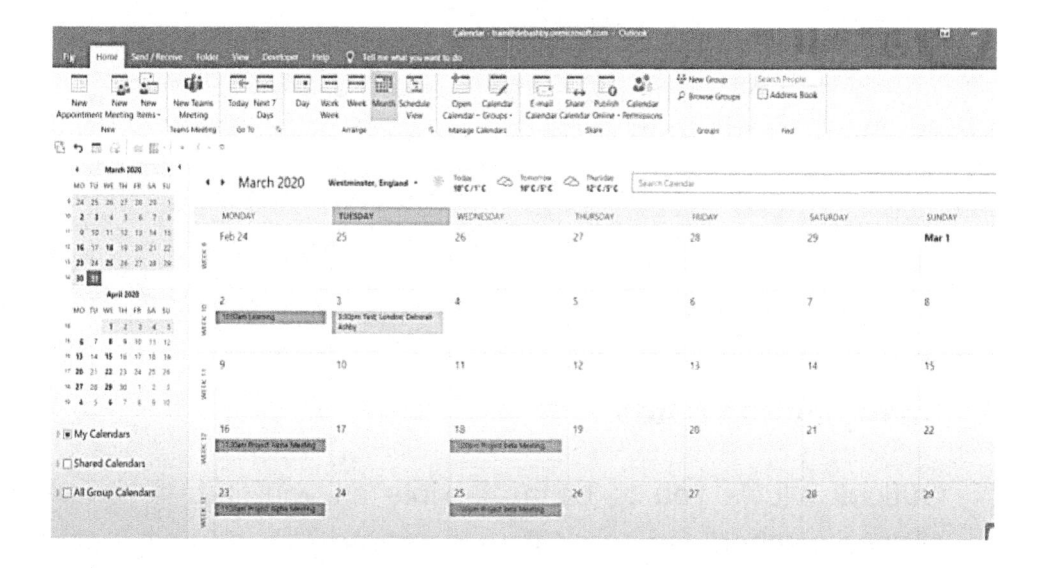

- Enter **a brief summary** of what the appointment is about in the Subject box.
  Put in a dental appointment, lottery winnings, or whatever you like. This will be displayed on your calendar.

- Enter **the address** in the Location box.
  If you include this step in your appointment, it is optional, but it might be useful information.

- Remember to include any other details about your appointment.
  You can save driving directions, meeting agendas, or anything else you might need to keep in mind when the appointment time arrives in the large, empty box on the Appointment form.

- Click on **the Save & Close button**.
  You will now see this appointment on your calendar. If you can't see your new appointment, you may need to click **the Date Navigator on the date it occurs**.

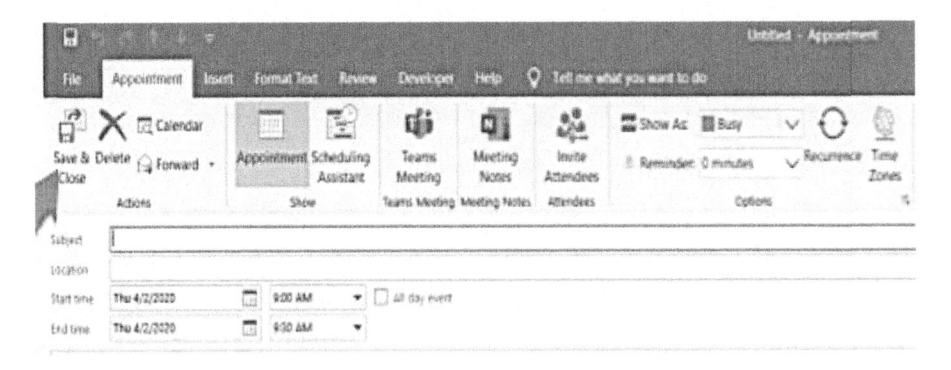

Changing the dates

Outlook allows you to be as flexible as you like. If you want to change a scheduled item's time, just drag it to the new location.

Follow these steps to change an appointment by dragging it:

- Click on **the appointment you wish to change** in the Calendar module.
  The appointment appears with a dark border around it.

- Ensure you're looking at Work Week, Week, or Month-one of the views that display times.

- To change the appointment time or date, **just drag the slider**.

Changing an appointment's date and time is also possible.

- **Double-click** the appointment in the Calendar module. An appointment window will appear.

- The selected month's calendar can be viewed by clicking the Calendar icon on the leftmost Start Time box. The calendar is displayed in a drop-down window.

- Select **a month** by clicking **one of the triangles** beside its name.
  You move one month earlier if you click **the left triangle**, and one month later if you click **the right triangle**.

- Click on **the date you want to view**.

- Enter **a new time in the Start Time text box**, if necessary. A new start time can also be selected **by using the scroll-down button**.

- If you need to make any other changes to the appointment, do so.

- You can change the information by clicking **it and typing over it.**

- Click on **Save & Close**.

Follow these steps to adjust the appointment length:

- Choose a Day, Work Week, or Week view of the appointment in the Calendar module.
  Due to the fact that you cannot see the time without opening the appointment, this process does not work on a monthly basis.

- By moving the mouse pointer, click **on the top or bottom handles of the appointment.**
  The pointer becomes a two-headed arrow when it is in the right place.

- Slide down the bottom line to extend the appointment time; slide up the bottom line to shorten it.

You can also make an appointment shorter than 30 minutes. The steps are as follows:

- Select the appointment by **double-clicking in the Calendar module**.

- Select **the "End Time" box**.

- Enter **the finish time**.

- Click **on Save & Close**.

Dates are being broken.

There are times when things just do not work out. It is unfortunate. Despite how hard it is for you to remember, Outlook erases dates that you otherwise cherish with a simple click. Actually, it takes two clicks. You can delete an appointment (after you've called to break it) **by following these steps:**

- Select **the appointment** from the Calendar module by **right-clicking**.

- Click **Delete**.
  Outlook will **cancel your appointment.**

   We've got to keep seeing each other: Recurring

After completing one thing, you're ready to tackle another. In Outlook, you can easily set up recurring appointments.

Follow these steps to schedule a recurring appointment:

- Select **the appointment** you'd like to repeat from the Calendar module.
  In the Ribbon, the Appointment tab becomes visible when an appointment is highlighted.

- On the Ribbon, click **Recurrence** on the Appointment tab.
  A dialog box appears.
  You would have the same appointment every week if you simply click **OK** in the Appointment Recurrence dialog box. It is possible that you won't be prepared for meeting scheduling indefinitely. It might be a good idea to fill out the rest of the Appointment Recurrence dialog box to be on the safe side

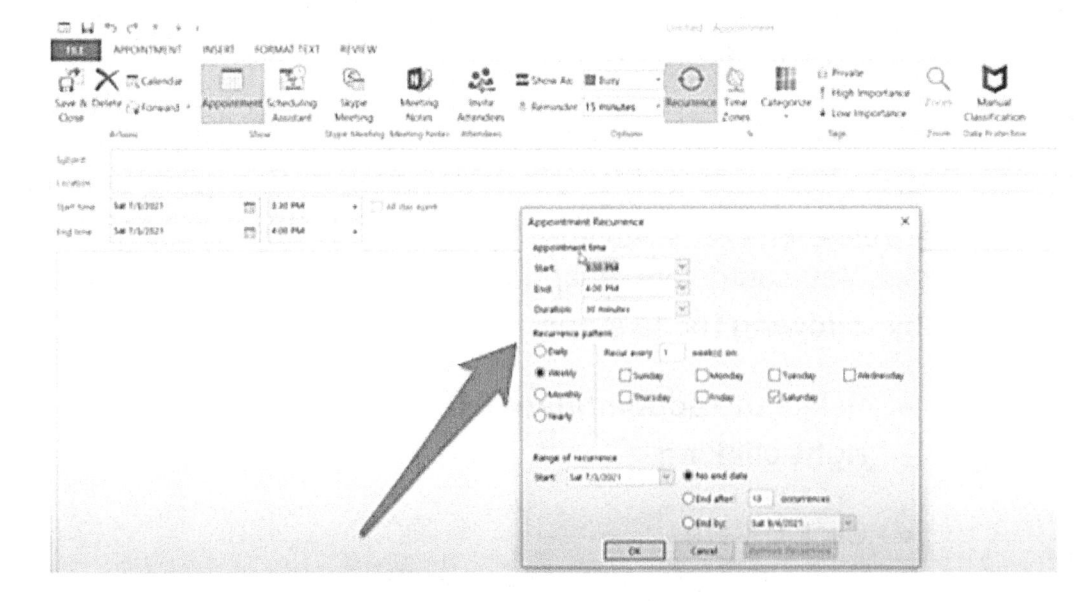

- Enter **the starting time in the Start text box**. The default time span for Outlook appointments is 30 minutes unless you specify a longer time span by entering an ending time. You can enter an ending time if you wish in the box labeled "End."

- You can choose **the recurrence pattern** for an appointment by clicking on the Daily, Weekly, Monthly, or Yearly option button under the Recurrence Pattern section.

- In the next section of the recurrence pattern section, specify how often the appointment occurs.

- Put the **first occurrence** into the start box of the Range of Recurrence section.

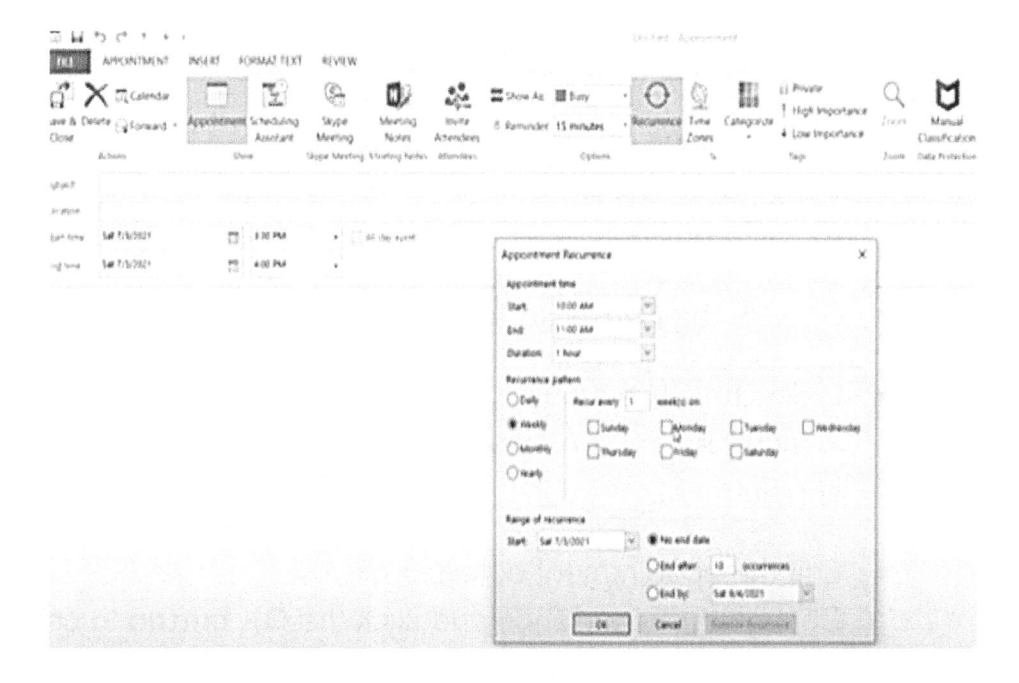

- Schedule the end of the appointments.
  Here are the options:

    - Endless (infinity)

    - Finally, After (a specific number of occurrences), It ends

    - on (a certain date)

- Click **OK** to confirm.
  A dialog box with Appointment Recurrences closes and the Appointments form appears.

- Enter **the subject in the Subject field**.

- Place your cursor in the Location box and enter the location.

- Click **Save & Close**.

Occasionally, a recurring appointment is changed as well.

You can edit recurring appointments as follows:

- **Double-click** on the appointment you wish to edit in the Calendar module.
  A dialog box entitled "Open Recurring Item" appears.

- Choose the **Entire Series**.

- Press the OK button.
  A recurring pattern appears under the location of the appointment.

- Edit the appointment details.
  Change the recurrence and click the **OK button** to change the pattern.

- Please click **the Save and Close button**.

Getting a Good View of Your Calendar

It is possible to organize the information in every section of Outlook virtually any way you can imagine—all by using varied views. The different ways to view a calendar could fill a cookbook, but I'll stick to the standard ways that most people see it. Outlook lets you make calendar arrangements nobody has ever thought of before. In the event that you accidentally create a calendar view, you don't like, you can delete it.

A calendar view consists of four basic views: the Day view, the Work Week View, the Week View, and the Month View. The Schedule view is useful for determining when things were done or when they will be done (such as when you did something and when you won't do something).

All of Outlook's calendar views are accessible from the Ribbon. To see a different view of the calendar, click on the name of the view you want. You can change the view at any time if the one you selected isn't suitable for you. You can arrange your calendar in a more streamlined vertical column by selecting the Schedule view. Other calendars can optionally be added (by clicking Add a Calendar) and their appointments compared hour-by-hour or day-by-day.

Printing Your Appointments

Plain old paper is still everyone's favorite reading material. You will probably need old-fashioned paper and ink to make your computer organizer truly useful, no matter how slick it is. Frankly, I've never been a fan of Outlook's calendar-printing feature. You are probably not to blame if you are unable to print your calendar correctly.

Any module in Outlook can be printed using the same basic steps. The steps are as follows:

- Click **on one of the dates** within the range of dates you want to print from the Calendar module.
  You can also print a single day by clicking on one date. You can pick a range of dates to print by clicking the first date, **holding down Shift,** and then clicking **the last date**. This highlights the entire range of dates you've selected.

- Select File, **then Print (Ctrl + P).**
  Printing controls are displayed.

- Choose **a style** from the Settings section.
  There are five basic options: daily, weekly, monthly, tri-fold, and calendar details. Outlook also lets you define your own

print styles, so you may eventually have quite a few options appearing here. The preview feature of Outlook lets you know what a page will look like before you print it.

- Press **the Print button**.
  You will get your dates printed.

Adding Holidays

What is the most important day of the week for workers? working days off! Calendar entries for major holidays can be automatically added to Outlook so you don't forget to take time off. You'd never know! Actually, Outlook can add holidays for over 70 countries as well as several major religions automatically.

You can add holidays to your calendar by following these steps:

- Navigate **to the File tab.**

- Select **options**.
  A dialog box appears with Outlook Options.

- Go **to the calendar.**

- You can add holidays to your calendar by clicking the "Add Holidays" button (under Calendar Options).
  A list of countries and religions will appear.

- You can add holidays by **clicking on them**.

- Once you have saved your changes, click **OK**.

- Please **click OK** once you have added the holidays.

- Close **the Outlook Options** window by **clicking OK**. Look up your holidays on the calendar.

Handling Multiple Calendars

It used to be regarded as thrilling and dangerous to lead a double life. Nowadays, they're considered underachievers. Get busy with your life, as you only have a small amount of time. It's easy to manage all your calendars with Outlook. Even if you're a mild-mannered person who is just trying to keep things calm, you might want to keep your personal and business calendars separate by setting up two calendars in Outlook.

Creating multiple calendars

The steps for creating another Outlook calendar are as follows:

- Click **on the Manage** Calendars tab on the Ribbon in the Calendar module to add a calendar.

- Create **a new blank calendar** by selecting **Create New**. A dialog box appears. It's like creating a new mail folder, but you're creating a new kind of folder that displays as a calendar.

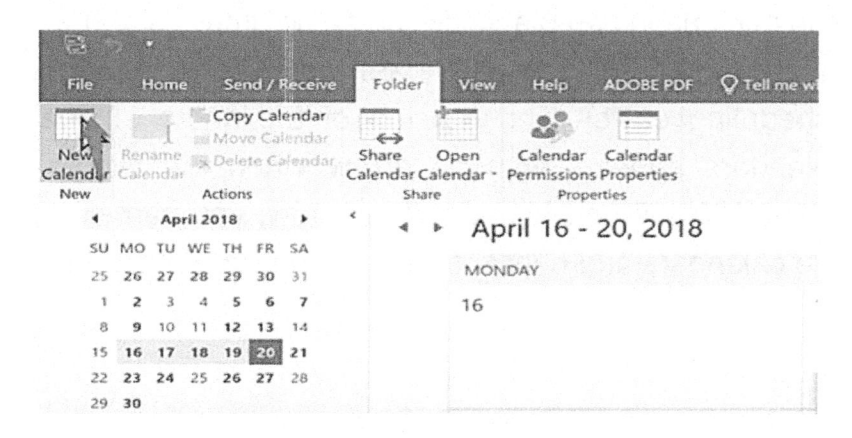

- Name **your new calendar** by clicking **the Name box**.

- Your new calendar's name appears next to a blank check box in the Folder pane as you click **OK**. Checking this box will allow you to view your new calendar alongside your original calendar in the Information Viewer, using the same day, week, or month view. To remove the checkmark, deselect the checkbox. The calendar you selected disappears.

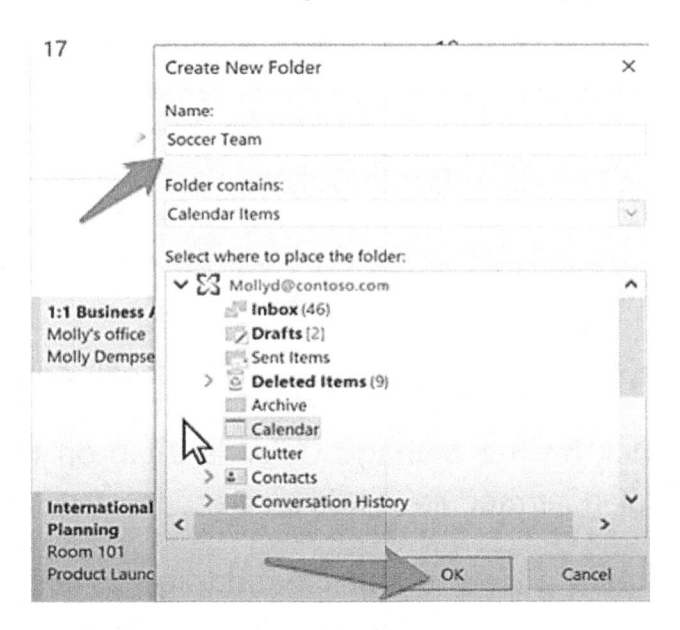

Managing multiple calendars

You can't be in two places at the same time. So you will appreciate the fact that Outlook calendars can be superimposed to make scheduling easier. The top tab of the name of one of the two calendars appears with an arrow when the two calendars are opened side by side. Using that arrow, you can superimpose the two calendars and check if any of your appointments clash.

CHAPTER 9

TASK MASTERY

In Outlook, you can store and manage more information about your daily activities than you might have wanted, but you'll find that it makes it easy to remember and keep track of your daily tasks. Organizing your tasks doesn't have to be a challenge in and of itself.

Entering New Tasks in the Tasks Module

You already have a full schedule; I don't intend to add more work to it. It's not so hard to add a task in Outlook. Outlook offers you lots of information about your tasks, but you can also enter a new task quickly and really quickly.

The quick-and-dirty way to enter a task

You can add a new task to your task list by clicking on the "Add New Task" button (or typing a new task, depending on the view you're using). Just follow the on-screen instructions. Using the regular, much slower way of entering a task is described in the next section if you can't see the box.

Here's how to get a task entered using the quick-and-dirty method:

- Click the **button that says "Click Here to Add a New Task"** (or type it in manually).
  It's written this way in the Detailed, Simple List, Prioritized, Today, and Server Tasks views; it's written this way in the

To-Do List views. These steps cannot be displayed in any other predefined view.

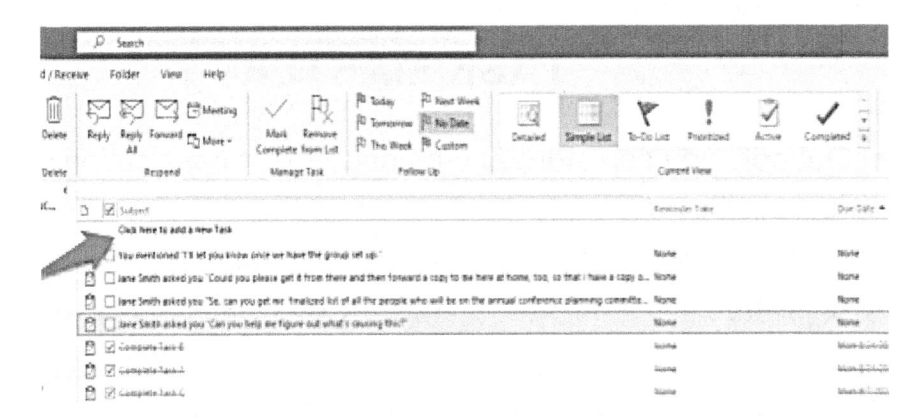

- Put **your task's subject** in the subject field.
  This will display your task's subject.

- You can now press **the Enter key**.
  That task will now appear as part of your task list.

The regular way to enter a task

Tasks are entered through the form, which takes a little more time to fill out but allows you to provide much more detail. You don't need to work your fingers to the bone to complete the task—if you enter a subject, you've completed it all. To add due dates and have Outlook remind you to finish what you've entered, you just need to fill out a few more boxes with your information.

To add a task to your task list, follow these steps:

- Click **New Task on the ribbon (or press Ctrl+N)** in the Tasks module.
  You will be presented with the task form.

- In the Subject field, type **the title of your task**.
  Make the subject one that makes it easy to remember what the task is about. Creating a task is mostly for the purpose of reminding yourself to perform the task.

- Click **the Start Date box** and enter **a starting date** to assign a start date to the task.

You can skip this step if you have not yet started the task. There is no need for a start date. It's only for your own use.

- For your task, you can enter **a due date** by clicking **the Due Date box** and choosing **a start date.**

As a default, it is just like the Start Date:

- If you want to choose the status of the task, click **the Status box**.
  Keep the status set to "Not Started" if you have not yet begun. Alternatively, you can select In Progress, Completed, Waiting on Someone Else, or Deferred.

- Choosing a priority can be done by clicking **the Priority box**. If nothing is changed, the priority remains normal. Other options include high and low.

- Optionally, check **the box next to "Reminder"** if you'd like to be reminded before the task is due.
  Leave the remainder blank if you want to forget the task. However, why do the task?

- If you wish, you may click **the date box** next to the Reminder checkbox and enter **the date when you want to be reminded.**
  In the Reminder box, Outlook automatically adds the date

you have entered. It is up to you which date you enter. When you choose **a date in the pas**t, Outlook informs you that no reminder will be set. There is a calendar on the right of the date box when you click the icon. You can choose **the date you want**.

- The time that you want to activate the reminder can be entered in the time field.
Set the time by **typing the numbers for the time**. Colon characters and other special characters are not necessary. Type 235 if you want to finish by 2:35 p.m. If you don't tell Outlook otherwise, it will schedule your appointments and tasks during daylight hours.

- Please **provide any additional information or notes** about this task in the text box.
  You can store directions, supply lists, or anything else you need for your appointment here.

- Finish by **clicking "Save & Close."**
  There is now a new task listed in your task list, awaiting completion.

Adding an Internet link to a task

In the Task form, typing the name of a website, such as www.facebook.com, sets the color to blue and makes the address a hyperlink you can click to open the website. You can easily save information about a great site by typing or copying the address into your task. Your web browser will open and display the page when you click on the text.

Editing Your Tasks

After you begin a new task, you are faced with the need to modify it immediately. Occasionally, I enter a task quickly and change some of the details later: A due date, a reminder, an extra step, etc. The task can be easily edited.

The quick-and-dirty way to change a task

Outlook offers an easy way to modify tasks in the same way it has an easy way to add tasks. Changing details is limited, but the process is quick.

Here are the steps you need to take if you can see the subject of a task and you want to make changes to the task you can see. For tasks or parts you cannot see, use the regular method, which I will describe in the next section.

You can change a task the quick-and-dirty way by following these steps:

- To edit a part of a task, highlight it and then click **on it.**
  This is especially useful if you want to edit the task's subject or due date. A blinking line appears **at the end of the text, a triangle appears at the right end of the box, or a menu appears**.

- Go to the old information. The **selected item is highlighted**.

- Fill out **the new information.**
  The old information will be replaced **by the new information**.

- Then press **Enter**.

The regular way to change a task

It is a little bit more difficult to change information about a task if it's not on the list you're viewing or if you don't want to be quick and dirty.

Following these steps will enable you to make changes the clean-and-long way (also known as the regular way):

- On the Ribbon, click **the Simple List view** if it is not already selected in the Tasks module.
  There are other views you can use if you know that they include the task you want, but Simple Listview is the simplest way to view your tasks; it's certain to include the task you're searching for.

- You can change a task by **double-clicking it.**
  Double-click **any component of the task**; it does not need to be its subject. You will be taken to the task form. From here, **you can modify anything in the box**.

- (Optional) Change the task's subject.
  Choosing a **subject** is up to you. Be sure to name it something that makes it easier to remember. The last thing you want is a computer telling you to do something you don't understand.

- Enter the **new start or due dates in the boxes under Start Date and Due Date, respectively (optional).**
  You can **choose from a variety of date styles**: 7/4/19, the first Friday in July, six weeks from now, whatever you like. I am afraid the 12th of Never is not available.

- The status can be changed by clicking **the Status box**, then **selecting a different status**.

- You can change the priority by clicking **the Priority box** and selecting **a new priority**.

- Optionally, you can turn the reminder on or off by **selecting or deselecting the Reminder check box**.
  They're simple and harmless, so why not take advantage of them? Make sure you get one now if you didn't ask for one the first time.

- Enter or change **the date for your reminder** by clicking **the calendar icon** next to the Reminder checkbox.
  Specify **any date** you like. There is no need to wait until the due date; you can submit it earlier, encouraging you to get started. Be sure to set it before the deadline. In general, the reminder will appear on the due date of the task.

- Enter **the time** when you wish to activate the reminder in the time box.
  Make **your entries** as simple as possible. You can use entry 230 to enter at 2:30 p.m. You can add or edit the instructions and notes in the text box.
  Detailed information can be added here that isn't really relevant elsewhere on the task form. It's only by opening the Task form again that you can see these details; normally, they cannot be seen in your Task list.

- Finish by **clicking "Save & Close."**
  That's it. Your task has been changed.

Deleting a task

Getting rid of tasks is the most satisfying part—ideally by completing the tasks you created. You can also delete tasks you no longer want. This version of Outlook isn't able to tell if you have finished any tasks, so you can delete anything you don't want to bother with.

Here are the steps for deleting a task:

- Select the **task** from the Tasks module.

- Select the **"Delete" button** from the Ribbon.

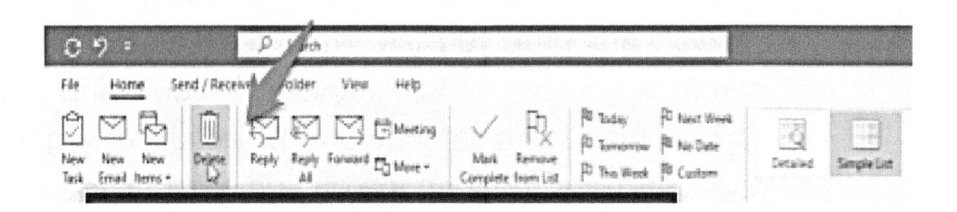

Alternately, you can press **the Ctrl+D or Delete key** on the keyboard. Everything is gone.

Managing Recurring Tasks

Tasks pop up frequently. When you have to do the same thing on different days, To save time and energy on entering tasks that you frequently do, you can set them up as recurring tasks. Outlook has the ability to bring it up again when it is time for the task to be done.

To create a recurring task, follow these steps:

- To open a task from the Tasks module, **double-click it**. Afterward, a form is opened.

- Press **the Ctrl+G shortcut key to recur** (or click **the Recurrence button** on the Task Form toolbar).
  You will be shown the recurring task dialog box.

- To specify how often the task occurs, select "daily, weekly, monthly, or yearly."
  You can **set a recurring monthly task** to take place at certain times of the month, such as on the 15th of every month or on the second Friday of every month.

- Recur Every lets you specify whether the task will repeat every month or every third day.
  In the case of creating a yearly task, you can set the task to recur each year on the same calendar day (such as the first Friday of June) or on a different day each month.

- Put **the first occurrence** into the start box of the Range of Recurrence section.

- There are several options to specify the end time of the task (No End Date, End After a certain number of occurrences, or End By a certain date).

- Press **the OK button**.
  There is a banner at the top of the task form describing how the task is repeated.

- Close the window by **clicking on "Save & Close."**

Once you've added your task to the list of tasks, you'll see a different type of icon than nonrecurring tasks, so you'll recognize that it's recurring. The icon for regular tasks looks like a tiny clipboard, but for recurring tasks, the icon appears as a tiny circular arrow.

Creating a regenerating task

Regenerating tasks behave like recurring tasks, except they reappear after a specified amount of time has passed since the last time they were completed.

If you use Outlook to schedule your lawn mowings, you can use Regenerating Tasks to generate your schedule. As far as I know, Outlook can't give you a rain forecast without a weather forecaster. Regardless, Outlook will help you keep track of whether you have actually mowed the lawn and make adjustments accordingly.

The steps for creating a regenerating task are as follows:

- **Double-click** the task to open it.
  A form appears.

- Press **Ctrl+G to activate the recurrence** option on the Ribbon.
  A dialog box will appear.

- Activate the option to regenerate new tasks.

- You can specify how long it should take for each task to be generated.

- Click **OK** to confirm.
  When you select a regeneration pattern for a task, a banner appears on the task form to describe it.

- Please **click the Save and Close button**.

Regenerating tasks have a different icon than non-recurring ones, so you are able to tell at a glance that they are recurring.

A regenerating task icon looks exactly like a recurring task icon, complete with that tiny circular arrow.

Skipping a recurring task once

In cases where you want to bypass just a single occurrence of a recurring task, there is no need to change the pattern of occurrence permanently; you may skip that occurrence and leave the rest alone.

Follow these steps to skip recurring tasks:

- To change a recurring task, **double-click it in the Tasks module**.
  A form is displayed.

- On the ribbon, click **Skip Occurrence.**
  It will change to the next scheduled occurrence date. There won't be a "Skip Occurrence" button if it's not recurring.

- Then click **the Save and Close button.**
  Regardless of the new occurrence date, the task will remain on your list.

Marking Tasks as Finished

There's nothing more satisfying than marking off completed tasks—and it's easier too. Right-click on the item you wish to mark as complete from either the To-Do bar or Task list and select Mark Complete. That's all there is to it.

Marking it off

Here are the steps for marking a task as complete:

- Activate the **Simple List view** in the Tasks module by clicking the **Simple List icon** on the Ribbon.
It doesn't matter which view you choose, as long as the task you want to find appears there. In the event that the task you want to mark as complete isn't in the view you selected, you might try the Simple List, which shows every task you've entered.

- You can mark a task as completed by **checking the box next to the subject.**
The box to the left of the second column is the one you want to choose. When the checkbox is selected, a line is drawn through the task subject. The task is complete.

By switching to the Completed view, you can see a list of the tasks you've marked as complete. It lists all the projects you've completed neatly and nicely.

There are several places in Outlook where tasks can be marked as complete. There is a task list as well as certain views of your calendar, as well as the task list within Outlook Today.

Picking a color for completed or overdue tasks

Upon completion of a task or overdue of a task, Outlook turns the text gray for completed tasks and red for overdue tasks, so you can see at a glance which tasks have been completed and which must be completed. In Outlook, you can choose different colors if you don't like the default colors.

You can change the color of completed and overdue tasks by following these steps:

- Click the **Options button on the File tab**.
  A dialog box appears with Outlook Options.

- Select **Tasks**
  A page with task options opens.

- Select the **Overdue Task Color**.
  A color palette appears.

- You can choose **a color** for tasks that are overdue.

- Select the "Completed Task Color" button.
  Colors will be displayed.

- Assign a color to completed tasks.

- Then click **OK**.

The tasks you complete and those that are overdue will appear in your list in the colors you select.

View Your Tasks

Task lists in Outlook can be viewed in several different ways, and a variety of custom views can be added and saved. If you know how to use Outlook's views, you can accomplish a lot.

You can select one of these views from the Current View group in the Ribbon to view your tasks:

- The detail view provides more information than the simple list view. The information is really the same, as is what the status of your tasks are, what percentage is complete, and what categories you assigned to your tasks.

- A Simple Listview shows only the facts. Each task's name and due date (if you assigned one) Add new tasks easily and mark old ones as complete using the simple listview. If more details are desired, no extra information will be displayed.

- Your To-Do List shows all the tasks you've entered along with any flagged emails. Only the items you have directly added to the task list are shown in the other views of the task list.

- Tasks are displayed in priority view according to the priority you have assigned to each task. Thus, you can see what's important and what's urgent.

- In Active view, you can only see tasks you haven't yet completed. Once a task is marked as completed, Active tasks vanish from the active view as they are completed, so you can focus on the tasks that remain.

- You'll see your completed tasks in the "Completed" view. Even though you don't have to deal with completed tasks anymore, you sure do feel a sense of satisfaction when you look at them.

- On the Today view is today's due and overdue tasks, which are essentially today's tasks! Getting a reminder of your workload is a great way to begin the day.

- Compared to Active, the Next 7 Days view appears to be more focused. The Next 7 Days view displays only tasks due to be completed within the next seven days. You'll like it if you like living in the moment.

- Your overdue view is a sign of naughtiness. These tasks should have been done yesterday, but they are still lingering today.

- Using the Assigned view, you can sort your tasks alphabetically by the name of the person you assigned each task to.

- If your company has a task server, you can view the tasks assigned through it. Among its fields are Assigned To, Custom Status, and Custom Priority, all of which are useful in collaborative situations.

Frequenting the To-Do Bar

The To-Do bar in Outlook makes it easy for you to keep track of the things you need to do by pulling them together in one place. Rather than forcing you to check your calendar, check your email inbox, and then check your task list, the To-Do bar makes it easy to see what you need to do at a glance.

Your to-do bar will usually include the following items:

- A list of tasks you've entered

- Several appointments have come up.

- Your flagged email messages are

To-do lists can be confusing at first, since things may appear there that you didn't put there directly. By applying the flag labeled "This Week" to a Monday email message, it will appear for action two Fridays later, even if you forgot that you sent it. To-Do bars keep you from forgetting that's what they're there for.

Adding a new item to the To-Do bar

On the Ribbon,

Click **the To-Do Bar button** and **pick Tasks from the drop-down menu** to display **the To-Do bar**. Besides tasks, you can also choose a calendar or people if you want this information displayed on the To-Do bar.

Right on **the To-Do bar is a box saying "Type a New Task."** Follow the instructions. When you're done, hit **Enter**.

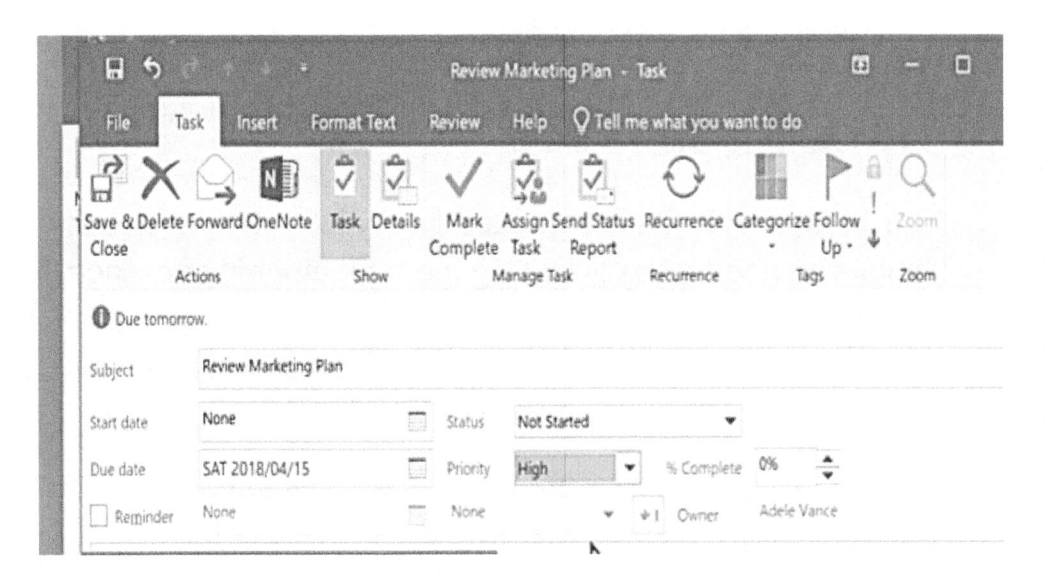

Tasks in the Calendar

Task lists and To-Do bars allow you to keep track of what needs to get done. When you have a free moment, you need to make sure you can do everything that needs to be done. To help you stay on top of upcoming tasks, Outlook displays a daily task list in your calendar. It can be accessed by clicking the View tab, clicking the Daily Task List button, and selecting Normal from the drop-down menu.

Across the bottom of the screen, you see a strip of icons that represent tasks whose due dates fall on the days displayed. When you have too many things on your to-do list for one day, just drag the task to a day when it can be completed. Tasks can even be dragged to a specific time in the calendar to reserve a specific time for completion.

CHAPTER 10

CUSTOMIZING OUTLOOK

"User interface" refers to the display of screens, menus, and other devices on your computer. It takes lots of effort and money for the people who write computer programs to figure out the best way to arrange things on the screen so that a program like Outlook is easy to use.

You can arrange and view the information in an endless number of ways in Outlook. An Organize button shows you the different ways you can slice and dice your Outlook data. Following the "Organize" button, this chapter contains many of the best steps you can take.

Customizing the Quick Access Toolbar

By keeping a few icons for your favorite functions at the top of the screen, the Quick Access Toolbar makes it convenient for you to use them anytime you want. When Outlook is freshly installed, only three Quick Access Toolbar icons are displayed: Send/Receive, Undo, and Customize Quick Access Toolbar. If you use Print, Delete, and so on frequently, you can customize the Quick Access Toolbar to include these functions.

Here are the steps to customizing the Quick Access Toolbar:

- Customize the Quick Access Toolbar by **clicking the icon**. This is located at the right end of the toolbar. The most popular Outlook functions are displayed in a drop-down menu.

- You can add a function by clicking **on its name**.
  A Quick Access Toolbar icon appears for the function you select.

Customizing the Ribbon

Several tabs make up the Ribbon, and each Outlook module has its own Ribbon, with its own set of buttons and tabs. It is not helpful to put a button in the wrong place on the ribbon.

Customizing the ribbon is as simple as these steps:

- Click on **any part of the ribbon**.
  An options menu appears.

- Select **"Customize the Ribbon."**
  A new window opens with Outlook Options.

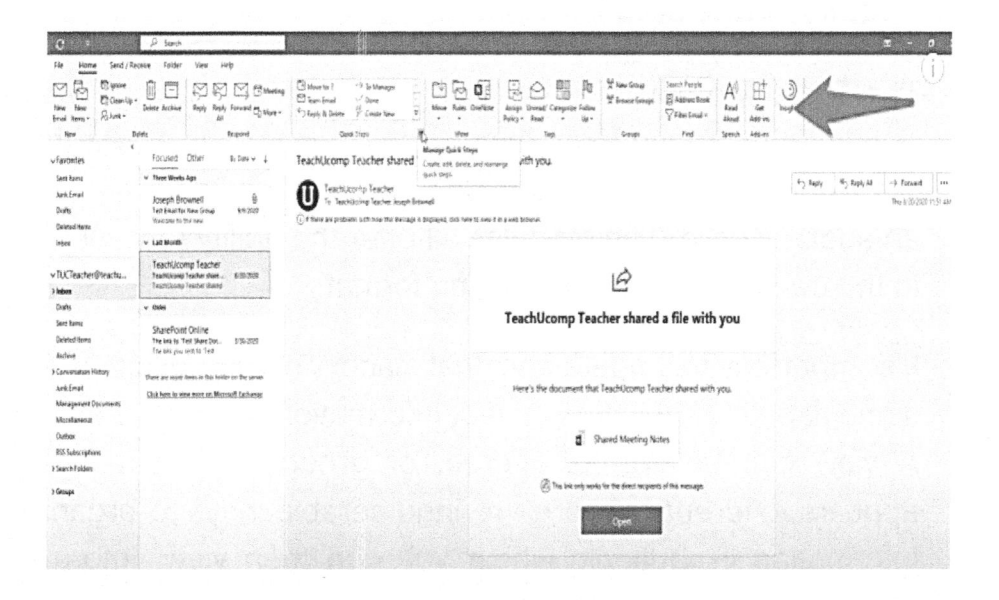

- Choose **the location** where you want the command to appear on or off the ribbon.
  The order of the buttons on the ribbon can be customized by dragging. When adding new commands to the Ribbon, click **on the New Group button** first and add the commands to the new group.

- Click the **OK button**.

The right-hand side of the screen has the commands that are already on the Ribbon. They can be removed if you wish. In the left-hand column, you can see the commands you might be able to add to the Ribbon. However, no command will be allowed to be added to the ribbon. In order to add a command to a ribbon, it must be appropriate for the module in which it appears. For example, the Mark Complete command can't be added to the Calendar Ribbon because it isn't useful there. This means that even if you try to add the command to this location, the Add button will be grayed out.

Taking in the Views

The Outlook modules each have their own selection of views and ribbon tabs. Among other things, the calendar has a view that looks like a calendar. Likewise, the Contacts module has a view similar to an address card. The modules all offer the ability to view your data in the traditional row-and-column format.

It's important to understand that each view is designed to make some aspect of how you collect information obvious at first glance. A view can be sorted, filtered, or grouped so that information appears differently. There are innumerable ways to organize your information in Outlook, which you can then view. Information is viewed differently depending on the kind you have and how you intend to use it. With views, there is no way to go wrong because if the old ones fail to work, you can easily make new ones. Experiment as much as you like.

Views usually have a name, which is usually found under the Current View section on the Ribbon. The Current View section may not appear under the Home tab. Click the View tab instead. There is a reason why Microsoft does not always place the Current View section in the same place on every module's Ribbon.

Table/List view

Each module has a table view—a rectangle with rows and columns. It is called the list view by some Outlook commands. As soon as you add a new item (such as adding a task to your task list), a new row appears in Table View. For example, the Tasks module's detailed view is a table view.

Card view

Card View is designed for the People module. Each contact item gets its own little block of information. Each little block shows a little or a lot of information about the item, depending on what kind of card it is.

Calendar views

Viewing dates and setting appointments on the calendar is a fantastic use of the calendar.

Using this module, you can easily switch between Day, Work Week, Week, Month, and Schedule Views from the Ribbon. Each of these views also shows a calendar for the month. A click on any of the dates will display the information for that particular date.

Playing with Columns in Table and List Views

Views based on tables (also known as lists) provide the most detail about the items you've created; you can also use these views to group information in the most efficient way. Despite their dull appearance, table views get the job done.

Information about each item is displayed in the columns of the table view. There is a great deal more data that can be stored in Outlook modules than you can display in a row-and-column format on your screen. In your contact list, for instance, you can access 90 different pieces of information about every individual. Each person would require more than 90 columns to display all their details if they were represented by just one row.

Adding a column

As a new user of Outlook, you only have a few columns in the Contacts list's Phone view. But if you wish, you can easily add more. There is no limit to the number of columns you can display, but the information may appear blurry as you scroll across the screen.

In any table view, you can add a column by following these steps:

- You can right-click **on any column title**.
  An option will appear.

- From the shortcut menu, choose **"Field Chooser."**
  A box with the Field Chooser appears.

- Place the **desired field** in the table.
  If the field you are looking for does not appear in the Field Chooser pane, select **All Contact Fields from the drop-down list at the top**.

- Close the **Field Chooser pane by clicking Close (X)** when you're finished, or leave it open in case you want to add more fields later.

Moving a column

It is easier to move columns than to add them. To move columns, just drag their headings. When dragging, you will see two little red arrows to indicate where the heading will end up when you release the mouse button.

Widening or narrowing a column

Columns can be narrowed or widened even more easily than they can be moved. To do so, follow these steps:

- The mouse pointer should turn into a pair of arrows when you continue to move it to the right edge of the column you want to widen or narrow.
  Making that mouse pointer look like a two-headed arrow requires skill. After a little practice, you'll realize how easy it is.

- By **dragging the column edge**, you can adjust its size. A thin line appears where the two-headed arrow is positioned, which can be dragged to resize the column.

Removing a column

If you do not wish to see certain columns, you can remove them. The steps are as follows:

- You can remove a column by right-clicking on **its heading**. An option will appear.

- Select **"Remove This Column."**

If you need to delete columns, don't worry about it too much. Once you remove the columns from the item, the fields remain. If you want it back, you can use the column-adding procedure I described earlier in this chapter.

Sorting Items

Sorting is just an orderly way of arranging your list. There is always an order to list. Changing the order is all that sorting does.

Your list can be sorted as follows:

- If a heading has a triangle, it means the list is sorted by the information contained in that column.

- The list goes down from the largest to the smallest number if the number is in the column and the high side of the triangle is at the top.

- The columns with text are sorted alphabetically. The letter A is the smallest, while the letter Z is the largest.

Sorting in the Table View

In my opinion, this is the easiest way. To sort a column in a table view, click the column heading. All the columns are sorted by what you clicked on; the date, the name, etc.

Sorting from the Sort dialog box

While selecting a column is the easiest way to sort, you can only select one column at a time. It is possible to sort by more than one column.

Here are the steps for sorting two or more columns:

- On the Ribbon, click **the View Settings button** and then select **the View tab**.
  Select Advanced View Settings from the dialogue box that opens.

- Select Sort from the menu. A sort dialog box opens.

- Pick **the first field** you want to sort by from the Sort Items By list box.

- Select carefully; there is a much longer list of fields in the list than is typically available in the view. The list may be confusing.

- You can sort either **by ascending or descending**.
  If you are sorting ascendingly, select smallest to largest. If you are sorting descendingly, select smallest to largest.

- Sort each field by **repeating steps 3 and 4**.

- Your list has been sorted. Click **OK**.

Grouping Items

There is a similarity between sorting and grouping. In both cases, items are arranged by column. In contrast to sorting, grouping creates a collection of related items that you can open or close. You can ignore all the other bunches and only examine those that interest you.

Viewing grouped items

A grouped view identifies the columns that were used to create that view. When choosing People and then List view (which groups your contacts by an organization), triangular icons appear on the left side of the screen. Because the view is grouped by company, it appears next to each icon. Next to the word "company" is the name of the company; the grouped view separates each company in the list.

A small icon appears at the left end of each group heading, either pointing directly to the right or downwards and to the right.

- When an icon points directly to the right, there's more to see; click it **to view these items**.

- With a triangle tilted down and to the right, there is nothing more to look at; what you see is what you get.

Choosing the company name without the icon selects the group as a whole.

By selecting the **company name** and clicking the **"Delete" button**, you can delete the group.

In order to distinguish a selected group bar from the others, it is **highlighted in blue.**

Viewing headings only

Alternatively, you can open or close all groups at once by clicking on each triangle individually.

Follow these steps for opening or closing groups:

- On the View tab, click Expand/Collapse.

- Either **collapse or expand the group**.

- By **choosing to Expand All Groups or Collapse All Groups, you can expand or collapse all the groups**.

Saving Custom Views

If you're used to saving Word documents, you're familiar with the idea of saving views. When you make any of the changes to the view I described earlier in this chapter, you can save the changes as a new view or save the changes to the current view. If you plan to use a certain view repeatedly, it's worth saving.

- Select **View from the menu**.

- Click **on the "Change View" button**.

- Select **the Save Current View option**.

- Give **your view a name**.

- By simply changing the views you already have, you can do almost anything you want.

Using Categories

Information collection is a valuable asset. If you can't quickly figure out which items are important and which aren't, then you can't get the most value out of a list of contacts or tasks. Outlook's "Categories" feature helps you quickly distinguish between urgent and non-urgent items.

Assigning a category

On the Mail module's Home tab,

Click the **"Categorize" button** in order to see what categories are available. The categorize button looks more like a small, colorful tic-tac-toe square.

When you click on the "Categorize" button, you'll see a list of color-themed categories. The process of changing the default color of items is fairly simple.

You can assign a category to an item by following these steps:

- If you would like to categorize a mail item, **click on it**. A highlight appears.

- Choose a category using the **"Categorize" button**. The item will appear colored according to the category you selected.

It is possible to assign multiple categories to each item, although choosing too many may lead to more confusion than choosing none at all.

Renaming a category

You can get an idea of what Outlook category colors mean to you, but I would prefer to know what each color means so I know why an item is in a particular category.

Follow these steps to rename a category:

- Select all **the categories under "Category"**.
  The dialog box for color categories appears.

- You can rename a category by clicking on it.
  Selecting **a category** highlights it.

- Rename **the file.**
  There is a box surrounding the category you selected to indicate that it may be edited.

- You can now rename the category.
  It is renamed after you type it.

- The dialog box for Color Categories closes after you click **OK**.

A category name you had previously assigned to some Outlook items will automatically change if the category name is changed.

Changing a category color

A category's color and name can be modified. Your ability to identify memorable colors can give you a good indication of how your work has gone or how well you've kept up with a project.

Changing a category's color is as simple as following these steps:

- Choose the **"All Categories"** option from the "Categorize" button.
  A dialog box appears.

- To change the color of a category, click **on the category name**.
  Your selected category will be **highlighted**.

- Select **a color** from the menu.
  You will see a drop-down menu with the colors you can choose from.

- Pick **a color** you'd like to assign.
  That color replaces the old one.

- The dialog box for Color Categories closes once you **click OK**.

Assigning a category shortcut key

Providing each category with a shortcut key allows you to assign a category without touching the mouse. Those tools are very helpful when you'd like a quick way to sort through a screenful of email messages.

Follow these steps to assign a shortcut key to a category:

- Choose **the "All Categories"** option from the **"Categorize" button**.
  A dialog box for color categories opens.

- A shortcut key can be assigned to a specific category by clicking **on it**.
  The highlighted category clearly shows you have selected it.

- The Shortcut Key drop-down menu box will appear. Shortcut keys will be listed there.

- To assign a shortcut key, click **the desired key**.
  Your shortcut key choice appears to the right of the category.

- The shortcuts can't be assigned to more than one category; it would be confusing. Individual items, however, can have more than one category assigned to them.

CHAPTER 11

SOCIAL MEDIA MAGIC WITH OUTLOOK RSS

Almost everyone uses social media these days. All these web services seem to have attracted a lot of attention, including Twitter, LinkedIn, and other popular ones. It is hard for most people to keep up with what is happening on social media; it changes far too frequently for them to keep up. For example, MySpace was the most popular internet destination in 2006. Since MySpace had become passé by 2009, I was assured by every tech expert that Facebook was the rage. It took only 30 months for MySpace to become yesterday's news. The only constant thing about social media is change. Young people are more and more transferring to Instagram and Snapchat as we speak.

However, social media isn't a passing trend. Business, culture, and public policy are being affected by social media trends. In the world of social media, no matter which particular service is dominant at a given time, you should keep at least a passing knowledge of what's happening since the developments could impact your career and business.

Brushing Up on Social Media Basics

With new social networks popping up and disappearing daily, it can be easy to get confused. In addition to keeping track of your social media subscriptions, Outlook can sync your email, contacts, appointments, and everything else you need to stay organized.

Sending an SOS to RSS

In Outlook, RSS stands for Really Simple Syndication, or Rich Site Summary, which allows you to keep track of all this changing information. You can organize RSS feeds in Outlook in a way that is useful to you by using Outlook's RSS folder. It isn't necessary to understand how RSS works, but knowing that it's available when you need it is nice.

A feed is a delivery method for RSS information. RSS feeds allow for the automatic updating of information over time. You can keep up with new entries and episodes by subscribing to RSS feeds offered by blogs and podcasts.

It might be necessary to make a few settings changes in Outlook in order for RSS to work.

The steps are as follows:

- Navigate **to the File tab in Outlook**.

- Select **options.**
  A dialog box appears with Outlook Options.

- Select **Advanced.**

- The Common Feed List (CFL) should be synchronized with RSS feeds using the Synchronize RSS Feeds box in the

Windows Control Panel.
Go to the RSS section.

- Then click **OK**.

If you're not a fan of Internet Explorer, Outlook is another way for you to subscribe to RSS feeds. (Windows includes it by default, so it is almost impossible for you to claim it isn't present. However, some people choose not to use it.)

Feeling like a social butterfly

We must not overlook the importance of blogs, podcasts, and news organizations as a part of the social media world. Although you may ignore any of them, it's highly likely that you're already reading or watching many of them.

Podcasts

Digital, downloadable editions of many radio stations' programs, including news, talk, and information stations like NPR, are available. Your favorite radio personalities often refer to these editions as "podcasts." These programs are typically scheduled regularly. Podcasts can be downloaded one at a time or automatically if you subscribe to them.

It is misleading to use the term "podcast." Podcasts are often thought to be compatible only with digital music players. Many people don't listen to podcasts as often as they would like because finding, downloading, and playing podcasts can be hard. In spite of the fact that podcasts were initially designed to play on portable devices, most people today listen to them on their computers. If you have Outlook installed on your computer, podcasts can also be played.

With Outlook, you can access any podcast that you've subscribed to and organize it using the same tools you use to manage email.

Blogs

Several years ago, everyone talked about blogs as if they were a brand new, magical technology, but they're not. If you surf the Internet for news and information, you might come across blogs without even realizing it. The majority of major news services feature a blog section where reporters and commentators discuss breaking news and current events. Blogs are nothing more than web pages that permit frequent updates and display the newest updates first.

Many people today prefer to get their news from bloggers. You can also waste a great deal of time if you surf one blog after another. Microsoft Outlook allows you to keep up with all your blogs in one place and stay on top of the latest gossip. It also keeps you up to date on important news.

Outlook can be used to read blogs, as well as feeds from news providers and more official-looking RSS sources.

Subscribing to an RSS Feed via Internet Explorer

Subscribing to blogs or other feeds is much easier with Internet Explorer than with Outlook. If you have a choice, Internet Explorer is the best place to go. Feeds you set up in either Internet Explorer or Outlook are accessible in both places for reading. In other words, you can set up RSS feeds in Internet Explorer and then have them read in Outlook.

RSS isn't supported by Microsoft's Edge browser.

These steps will allow you to subscribe to a blog or another RSS channel in Internet Explorer:

- Using Internet Explorer, navigate to the RSS feed page for the blog or news source you wish to subscribe to.

- You can subscribe to this feed by clicking the Subscribe to This Feed hyperlink on the page.
  Alternatively, you can follow these steps:

    - To access favorites feeds, and history, click **the start button** (top-right corner of the browser window).

    - A task pane appears.

    - In the task pane, select **the Feeds tab**.

    - Select **"Add to Favorites"** from the drop-down menu.

- The dialog box for subscribing to this feed opens.

- Press **the Subscribe button.**
  Click **OK** to close the dialog box.

Internet Explorer and Outlook can now display the feed.

When you subscribe to a new blog, an RSS Feed folder shows the blog's name in the Outlook Folders list in the Navigation Bar. All you need to do is check the folder. The RSS Feeds folder might need to be expanded to see your newly subscribed content.

Setting Up an RSS Feed in Outlook

As I mentioned earlier, if you use Internet Explorer or Outlook, you can set up any RSS feed and then access it from either. However, it is probably best to use the Outlook method, however, if you are subscribing to a podcast. That way, you can configure the feed's settings while you are there.

Setting up a podcast, or an RSS feed of any type, in Outlook can be done in the following manner:

- Choose **Account Settings** from the Account Settings menu when you click **the File tab.**
  A dialog box appears.

- Select **"RSS Feeds"** from the menu.
  Subscribed feeds appear on the RSS signup page.

- Press **the New button**.
  A dialog box opens to let you create a new RSS feed.

- Your RSS feed URL should be entered here.
  URLs like this usually look unusually long.
  http://www.cinemasolo.com/atom.xml Incorrectly entering the address will result in an error.

  Here are the steps you should follow:

    ○ Find the feed you want on the site where it is hosted.

    ○ Choose XML, RSS, or Feed from the right-click menu. Depending on the site, this could be an orange button or a button that looks like the wireless network icon in the notification area.

- ○ Select **"Copy Shortcut"**.

- ○ As soon as you have pasted the address, you can follow the preceding steps and add a new RSS feed.

- Click on **the Add button**.
You can make the following changes to your RSS feed subscription using the RSS Feed Options dialog box:

    - ○ **Feed Name:** The name shown by Outlook can be changed. Feed names can be complicated.

    - ○ **Deliveries:** Some feeds generate large amounts of information, so you may want to send that information to a special folder or to a completely separate file. Podcasts are a good example. If your company has a limit on the amount of email storage you can have, you might want to save your RSS subscriptions to a separate Outlook account so that you don't run out of space.

    - ○ Using Outlook's automatic download feature, Outlook only downloads a brief summary of each item. This saves disk space, but you must manually download the full text of each item if need be.

    - ○ By selecting **the Download Enclosures checkbox**, the podcast file and the description will be downloaded.

    - ○ The RSS feed publisher may have a limit on how often your information can be updated. Subscriptions that are updated too often may be canceled. There is an automatic checkbox marked "if there is a limit assigned to the feed you have selected."

- You can now click **OK**.

- Close this window.

Reading Feeds

The RSS feeds aren't visible from the navigation pane, so you have to open the RSS folder. Reading RSS feeds takes a few extra steps, but once you find your way to the RSS folder, it's pretty simple.

In Outlook, you can read RSS feeds by following these steps:

- On the navigation bar, click **the Mail button.**
  You will see a list of your mail folders.

- Select **the RSS Feeds folder** by clicking **the arrow**.
  RSS feeds are displayed in the folders. There is one feed per folder. A triangle next to RSS Feeds indicates you have not yet set up any RSS feeds.

- You can now read the feed by clicking on **the folder that contains it.**

Upon subscribing to one or more podcasts and choosing automatic downloads, double-click the attachment in the message file. You will be able to listen to your podcast after your computer launches a player.

CHAPTER 12

MANAGING MULTIPLE EMAIL ACCOUNTS

One email address is common among many people. Once they install the program or someone else does it for them, they set it up in Outlook. Nevertheless, you are not that many people, otherwise, you wouldn't be reading this chapter. You crave more flexibility, more privacy, more small business sidelines, maybe even the ability to use a secret alter-ego like Freaky4U@FantasiesComeTrue.biz on the down-low. The purpose of this chapter is to demonstrate how to set up additional email accounts in Outlook and to provide some advice on how to get those email addresses from various services.

Choosing an Email Provider

The majority of people who have computers at home have an Internet service provider (ISP). Your Internet provider is the one you pay a monthly fee to. ISP options may include your cable provider, telephone provider, or satellite provider, depending on where you live.

Oftentimes, when people get their first Internet connection, they receive an email account from their ISP. It's free and easy for them, and they don't know any better.

Most ISPs provide free email accounts with their ISP services. The setup for their email is usually very straightforward. Every family member can have a personal email address. In fact, they want to be both your email provider and your Internet service provider for free! Don't they sound too good to be true?

You may not be able to shop around for better ISP deals later if you take advantage of this offer. If you have an address with an ISP and have been sending emails from that address for a year or more, changing to a different ISP becomes more difficult since you must notify everyone you know of your new email address. Trying to remember all the merchants and services you used that email address for can be overwhelming because you've probably forgotten all the accounts you created with them. It's so much trouble to have to change email addresses that you'll be stuck with that ISP no matter what their prices are.

Many different services offer free email addresses as an alternative to getting your own address. You can use Gmail from Google, for example, and Microsoft's Outlook.com is free. Microsoft's Office 365 plans also provide a range of options, from basic plans for private users to sophisticated plans for large multinational corporations.

Another popular option is email service provider Mail.com (www.mail.com). Mail.com lets you register for a free email address and check your messages online. In order to use the robust mail-management capabilities of Outlook, you'll have to upgrade to a POP3 or an IMAP account on Mail.com, which will cost you an extra fee per year.

Buying Your Own Domain Name

With a domain name, you can have as many email addresses as you want. You can get one for about $30 a year (maybe a little less). You could, for example, buy the domain roblevsky.com and set up the address Mordecai@Roblevsky.com if your name is Mordecai Roblevsky. Using your first name as an email address might not be possible if you have a more common name, such as John Smith. If need be, you can either change your name or use a variation of your name.

The process of purchasing your own domain consists of three steps:

- **Register the domain name.**

    It must be an available name, of course. Payments can be made just for one year, or several years ahead of time. The cost ranges between $5 and $20 for this service. A domain registrar handles this for you. The most popular is GoDaddy, but there are others as well. A domain registrar manages your contact information and your ownership of the domain name. Well, you are essentially renting it, so long as you keep paying for it. It is yours to use however you wish.

- **Sign me up for hosting.**

    Hosting is defined as the service that manages your domain's web and email servers. When people enter your domain name in their browser, your hosting company will direct their web traffic to the website associated with your domain. Additionally, your domain can also be set up to send and receive emails through the host's email servers. Hosting can be provided by the same company as the registrar (and admins find this method easier), or a separate company can be used.

- **Create the email accounts.**

    You can create email accounts and assign passwords to them through the control panel of your hosting company. The accounts can be whatever you wish. You can type anything before the @ symbol. Your domain name follows the @ symbol. Taking this example, Mordecai could set up email accounts for everyone in the Roblevsky family: levi@roblevsky.com, toby@roblevsky.com, and so on.

Setting Up Email Accounts in Outlook

Using Outlook, you can send and receive emails from your new email account once you've signed up for one. The new account you set up will coexist with your existing Outlook email account.

Understanding POP3 vs. IMAP

POP3 and IMAP are two protocols for accessing email accounts, including those you create with your own domain and those you get from your ISP. An email account using a web interface must support POP3 or IMAP in order to integrate with Outlook. In some cases, you can choose between the two.

IMAP uses a server to store all your messages, and your local email client updates your mail folders as soon as you connect to the server. Deleted messages in Outlook are also deleted from the server copy of your inbox. If you use this system on multiple devices, each will show you the most up-to-date version of your email. Each device will display the same version of your inbox. If you use multiple devices to check your email, including a desktop, tablet, or smartphone, then this is the account for you.

When you use POP, however, the focus is on your local PC and email client (for example, Outlook). Sending and receiving messages over POP3 mail servers transfers new messages directly to the local PC without being accessed by the server. Outlook can be configured to delete or save transferred messages as a backup immediately, but the server doesn't check whether a message has been read or responded to.

A desktop computer was probably the only computing device that most people had back then. POP3 dates from the 1990s and was designed for a time when most people had just one device. It does, however, have some advantages. It is possible, for example, to access your old messages from your computer at any time, even if the Internet is not available. Due to your old emails being stored locally rather than on the server, you won't need to worry about the email server storage limit ever being reached. It is also possible to combine the incoming email from two or more POP3 accounts into a single Outlook data file, allowing for easier backups and file transfers.

Almost all email systems that support one of these also support the other, so you can specify which you want. When setting up an account in Outlook (or whatever email client you are using, such as the mail app on your smartphone), you are free to make a choice. You can choose in accordance with your needs.

Collecting the needed information for setup

Setting up an email account using default settings in Outlook isn't difficult; you only need an email address and password. The rest can usually be handled by Outlook. It's easy to set up an email account in Outlook 2019 compared to previous versions, so if you haven't done so for a while, you are in for a pleasant surprise. You can start there if you aren't a techie.

However, if you think you may need to change your email account settings, or if you just want to be proactive, **contact your email provider in advance:**

- email address and password. You don't have to think about it. They are required.

- **incoming mail server address.** This address is formatted as text.text.text. Probably in the form of imap.secureserver.com or pop.secureserver.com. Depending on whether you have your own mail server or not, the second and third parts of that might be the same as your domain name.

- Outgoing mail server address It is also formatted as text.text.text. You might see it as SMTP-out.secureserver.com. In the first slot, you will likely see the letters SMTP.

- SMTP stands for Simple Mail Transfer Protocol. Email is sent using SMTP. (POP3 and IMAP provide mail receiving capabilities.)

- Port numbers are used to receive and send mail.

- What encryption method does the server require for encrypted connections?

- For either sending or receiving, the server must use Secure Password Authentication.

Most providers have a support section on their website where you can find this information. To get the correct spellings of the server names and passwords, contact the tech support department of your online service or ISP. (Be sure to ask if they're case-sensitive, which means capitalization is important!)

Setting up an account using automatic settings

As I mentioned above, Microsoft Outlook 2019 makes it easy to set up accounts without having to provide too much technical information. This method works well for people who don't need to mess with settings when setting up their accounts.

These steps will allow Outlook to detect and configure the correct settings for a new Internet email account:

- Navigate to **the File tab.**
  A backstage view appears.

- Select **Account Settings** from the drop-down menu by clicking on **the Account Settings button.**
  A dialog box opens.

- If it isn't already selected, click **the Email tab**.
  A page for setting up email accounts appears.

- Select "New" **from the menu.**
  A new account dialog box appears.

- Click **Connect** after entering the email address for the account you wish to set up.
  Upon entering **your email address**, Outlook will attempt to automate the setup.

- In the Password box, enter the account's password and click **Connect**.
  Outlook then attempts to configure your email account automatically. When it succeeds, a box appears titled "Account Successfully Added." If it doesn't work, close all the dialog boxes and try again by following the instructions in the next section.

- Complete the process by clicking **the Done button**.

Setting up an account using manual settings

In most cases, Outlook hides from you the complicated mail settings you can specify for your account, as you saw previously. As such, if you are able to set up your email account on Outlook and ignore all those settings, that's wonderful.

Should the automatic method fail, here's what you should do next:

- Navigate **to the File tab**.
  You will see the backstage view.

- You can change your account settings by clicking **the Account Settings button** and selecting **Account Settings**.
  A dialog box opens with account settings.

- If you haven't already selected **the Email tab**, click **it now**.
  A page for configuring email accounts appears.

- Select **the "New" button**.
  The Add Account dialog box opens.

- Enter **the email address** for the account you wish to create.

- Select **"Advanced Options."**
  You will see a box that says "Let Me Set Up My Account Manually."

- Click **Connect** after checking the box.
  The advanced setup appears with icons for various email accounts, including Office 365, Outlook.com, Exchange, Google, POP, and IMAP.

- Set up a new account by clicking **on the appropriate type**.

- When prompted for a password, type it and click **Connect**. A screen will appear stating that the account was added successfully.

- **Try any of these:**

    o Enter **another email address** in the Add Another Email Address box, click **Next**, and follow the prompts to set up the new account.

    o Setting up **Outlook** for my mobile phone, too, will send you an email with the link to set up this email address there. A page with instructions will be displayed.

    o Click **Done** to complete the process.

- Click **"Close"** when the Account Settings dialog box appears.

Modifying Mail Account Settings

You can edit the settings of any of the mail accounts that are set up in Outlook. Changing the password for an account on the server (such as if someone got access to it and you need to change it for security reasons) might require changing the stored password.

You can modify an account's settings by following these steps:

- Navigate **to the File tab**.
  You will see the backstage view.

- Select **Account Settings from the drop-down menu**.

- If you haven't already selected it, click **the Email tab**. The Email Accounts setup page appears.

- A page for setting up email accounts appears.

- Click on **Change** when you have selected an account to modify.

A dialog box for changing accounts opens:

- Edit the account details if necessary.

- Then click **Next**.

- Click **the Done button**.

- Click **Close to close the Account Settings window**.

Changing the Mail Server

When you struggle to access an email account, a technician at your ISP may suggest that you change the port or address assigned to your mail server.

Previously, Outlook made this fairly simple, but not anymore! In order to prevent people like us from messing around with those settings, they dumbed them down.

Even so, there is still a way forward. Instead of the change command, use the repair command.

This is what you need to do:

- Navigate **to the File tab**. A backstage view appears.

- Click **the Account Settings button** and choose **Account Settings from the drop-down menu**.

- A dialog box opens with account settings.

- If it isn't already selected, click **the Email tab**.

- A page for setting up email accounts appears.

- Click **"Repair"** after selecting the account to modify.

- The Advanced Options page will appear.

- If you want to manually repair your account, select this checkbox.

- Click **the repair button**.

- A dialog box with account settings appears.

- The settings for incoming mail are displayed first.

- If necessary, edit the incoming mail settings.

- You might change the mail server or port number, the password, or the encryption algorithm, for example.

- Click **the Outgoing Mail tab**.

- You will see the settings for outgoing mail.

- Change the outgoing mail settings if necessary.

- You might, for example, change the outgoing mail server or port number, the server timeout delay, and whether authentication is required for SMTP.

- Click **the repair button**.

- Click **the Done button**.

Sending Messages from Different Accounts

When you have multiple accounts set up, Outlook adds a new button to the message composition screen. When you click **"On Form,"** you will be able to select your account from which to send the message.

Email messages are always sent from the default account. It may not always be obvious which account should be used. It is sometimes selected as the one that is most frequently used.

Follow these steps to change the default account:

- **Navigate to the File tab**.

- A backstage view will be displayed.

- Select **Account Settings** from the drop-down menu by clicking on **the Account Settings button**.

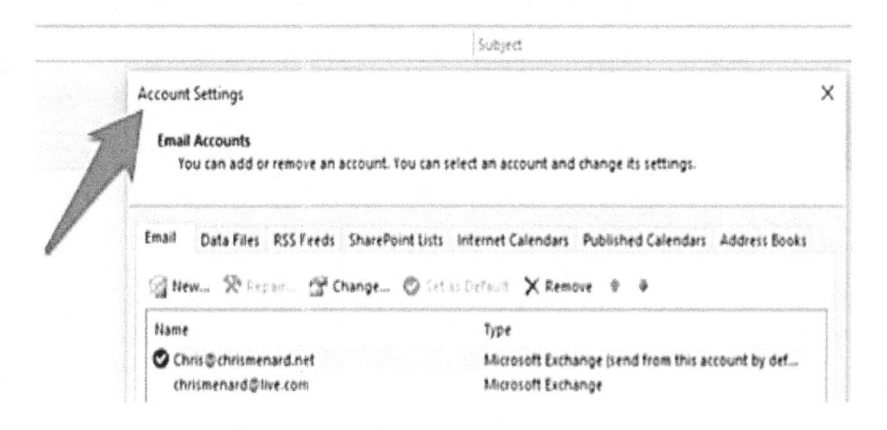

- A dialog box opens with account settings.

- Ensure that the Email tab is selected if it is not already selected.

- A page for setting up email accounts appears.

- Select **the default account.**

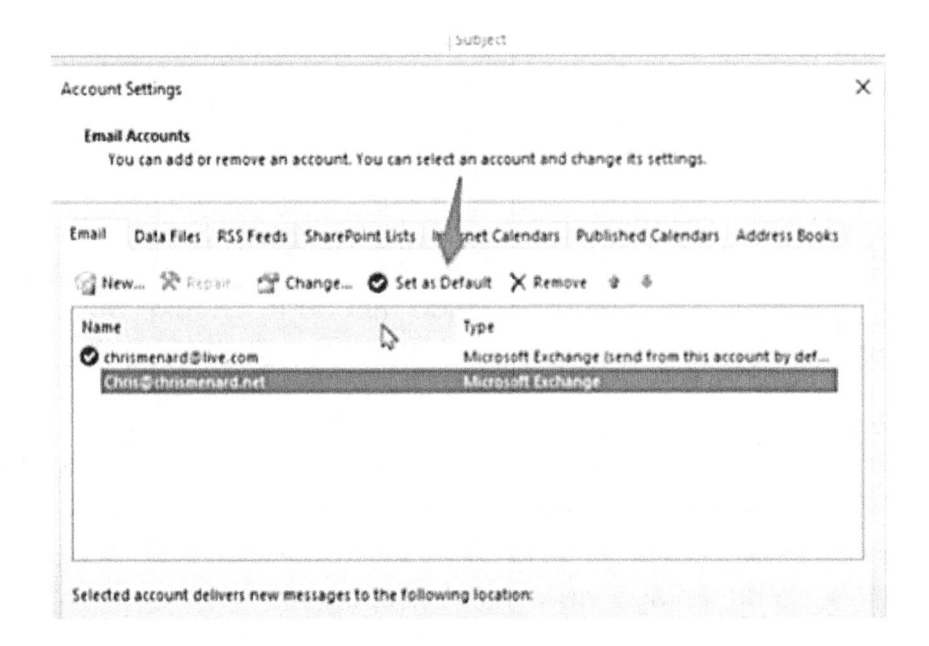

![Account Settings window showing Email Accounts tab with two accounts: chrismenard@live.com (Microsoft Exchange - send from this account by default) and Chris@chrismenard.net (Microsoft Exchange) highlighted. An arrow points to the "Set as Default" button.]

- Set it as the default by clicking **on it.**

- Click **Close** to close the Account Settings window.

CHAPTER 13

MERGING MAIL FROM OUTLOOK TO MICROSOFT WORD

In case you're not familiar with the concept of mail merge, it's a way of creating a letter on a computer and then printing different copies of it to different people. It's more than likely you get many merged letters every day. It's called "mail merging" when you send a mass mailing. Junk mail is when you receive a mass mailing.

Making Mailing Label Magic

There is a possibility that you may want to send a message to all of your friends to inform them about a party or a meeting. Hence, mailing labels can be created instantly for everyone on your contact list. Word's Mail Merge feature allows you to integrate the list into itself, so you won't have to worry about exporting files or determining where they went.

Urging merger

Verify that your printer is set up with the correct labels. Next, create your mailing labels by following these steps:

- Go to **the navigation bar** and click **"People."**
  A list of your contacts appears.

- In the Actions group of the Ribbon, click **the Mail Merge button.**
  Hence, the Mail Merge Contact dialog box opens.

- Select **Mailing Labels from the list** of document types in the Merge Options section.

- From the Merge To list, select New Document.
  This should already be selected but ensure you verify it.

- Click **OK to confirm**.
  The Mail Merge Helper dialog box opens in Microsoft Word. It tells you that Outlook has created a mail merge document and that the document needs to be set up by clicking **the setup button.**

- Then click **the OK button**.
  A dialog box will open.

- Click on **the Setup button**.
  The Label Options dialog box opens.

- Choose **a label brand** from the Label Vendors drop-down menu.
  Avery is one of the most popular label brands; generic labels often list an Avery product number equivalent on their packaging.

- Choose **the label product number in the Product Number drop-down menu**.
  Check the stock number on your label to make sure it's the same as the one you're choosing. If the stock number isn't available, you can look at the label dimensions in the Label Information section of the Label Options dialog box.

- Click **OK**.
  The Label Options dialog box closes.

- Click **the Close button** in the Mail Merge Helper dialog box.
  The Mail Merge Helper dialog box closes.

- From the Mailings tab of the Ribbon, click the Address Block button.
  A dialog box appears.

- The dialog box will close once you click **OK** to accept your settings.
  A funny-looking code appears in the first table cell and further down in the table cells: **AddressBlock > > and **Next Record > >. This is known as a "merge code," and it tells Microsoft Word which details to include in your document.

- From the Ribbon, select **Update Labels**.
  As a result, Word now displays the **AddressBlock > code along with **Next Record > » in every cell of the table, showing that it knows how to fill your label page with addresses.

- You can preview the results by clicking **the "Preview Results"** button on the ribbon.
  Word displays how the document will appear when printed. If the preview looks good, you can proceed.

- In the Ribbon, under the Mailings tab, click **the Finish & Merge button** and then select **Edit Individual Documents**. The Merge to New Document dialog box opens, which allows you to print part of the addresses or all of them in your document. If you choose "all," then the entire range will be printed.

213

- To proceed, click the **OK button.**
  The labels have been created.

- To print your labels, select **the File tab and then Print**.

Making and using a merge template

The blank label document can be saved and used repeatedly if you often print labels.

Here is what you need to do after you've created your labels:

- Go back **to the document that contains the merge fields**. A document begins with the name of the file, whereas a label begins with the name of the label's output file. Until Preview Results is disabled, its contents look much like the Labels file; select Preview Results to disable Preview Results, and you will once again see the merge codes "Next Record" and "AddressBlock."

- You will need to click **File**, then **Save As**.
  A Save As screen will appear.

- Go to the Browse tab.
  You can enter **the file's name** and location in the Save As dialog box.

- Find the **location** where you want to save the file.
  You will need to do this only if you want to change the default location for saving the file.

- Put the name of the document in the File Name text box. Choose a name that will stay in your memory, like the clever Blank Labels.

- Save the file.
  When the Save dialog box closes, the file is saved.

- Save any remaining open files, and then close Word.

Try this abbreviated procedure the next time you want to do a mail merge:

- Navigate **to the People tab**.
  You will see a list of your contacts.

- From the Ribbon (under the Home tab, click the Actions group), select **Mail Merge**.
  A dialog box appears, titled **"Mail Merge Contacts."**

- Select **Mailing Labels** from the list of document types in the Merge Options section.

- Choose **"Existing Document"** as an option in the Mail Merge dialog box.

- Select **Browse from the menu.**

- Click on **"Blank Labels" twice**.

Streamlining the mail merge process eliminates a lot of steps, so you can move on to more interesting tasks, such as stuffing envelopes.

Understanding Formal Letter Formalities

It's a letter with standardized text that's repeatedly printed, but with a different address and name on every copy. Regardless of whether you are holding a sweepstake, form letters are still appropriate. One form letter you could write is an annual newsletter to your family and friends.

The following steps will guide you through the process of creating a form letter in Outlook:

- Select **people** from the navigation bar.
  A list of your contacts appears.

- Go to **the Home tab** of the Ribbon and click **Mail Merge**.
  A new dialog box opens.

- Select **"Form Letters"** under the Document Types menu.

- In the Merge To list, select **New Document**.
  The option should already be selected, but it is worth checking.

- Click **OK** to open a blank document in Microsoft Word.

- Fill in the blanks on the form letter.
  It's up to you whether to type the generic parts of the letter first.

- Place the mouse pointer where the merge field should appear.
  You can, for example, type "Dear", followed by the first name of the person.

- In the Mailings tab of the Ribbon, click **the Insert Merge Field button** and then select the field you want to merge. Field lists consist of every field Outlook can store for each contact. Of course, not every contact will have the same information in every field, so focus on the core fields for consistent results.

- You can check your work before saving the letter and printing it, just as you did with the labels.

With this, you can send a personal, annoying form letter to hundreds of people instead of sending impersonal, annoying form letters to dozens of people.

Merging Contacts from Selected Lists

A letter to everyone on your contact list is probably not necessary. The postage alone could cost a fortune if you end up with thousands of names on your list. If you only intend to send letters to a few contacts, limit your list to just a handful.

You can add people to Outlook by opening the People module and clicking on the first person you would like to add. Press and hold the Ctrl key and select each person you want to include. Use the Mail Merge button and create the merge as you learned in earlier sections of this chapter.

You'll Still Have to Lick It: Printing Envelopes

If you are sending a mass mailing, it is not necessary to print labels; just print on the envelopes. You may even have an envelope feeder on your printer. It's tedious to feed envelopes one by one.

Following the steps I described in the earlier section for creating mailing labels, you can print addresses directly on your envelopes. The main significant difference is that in the 8th step, a dialog box titled "Envelope Options" appears that offers several options for envelope sizes. You'll need to decide which type of envelope you're using (generally, the standard business envelope number 10) and then follow the remaining steps.

Email Merging

Merging emails is another appealing feature of Mail Merge. If you want to send a bulk email message to a bunch of people and customize each message, you can use mail merge email. In most cases, you don't need to use merge email because you can send a single message to as many people as you want. So, Paul, George, and Ringo will not get your "Dear John" message.

In the section "Mastering Formal Letter Formalities", follow steps 1–3. At the fourth step, select Email (rather than New Document) from the Merge To list in the Mail Merge Contacts dialogue box.

With Outlook on an Exchange server, the document is sent directly to your recipient after you click Finish & Merge. It's impossible to fix something you've done wrong. To make sure that your email merge works,

I recommend sending yourself an email first:

- Click **on your name** in the Contacts list to create your merge message. After you're sure what you want to say has been expressed.

- Select **all the people** you wish to contact and merge the list.

As a user of Outlook at home, you can disconnect from the Internet temporarily before merging, after which you can switch to your Outbox and approve the collection of messages.

CHAPTER 14

BIG-TIME COLLABORATION WITH OUTLOOK

There is no question that Microsoft writes big programs for big companies that have a lot of money. As you'd expect, Outlook used to be geared more towards employees at big companies. These days, small businesses also require tools to enhance collaboration and teamwork. In an age of remote virtual teams whose members mainly communicate via phone and email, this is especially relevant.

Most companies that use Outlook usually have a server running in the background called Microsoft Exchange Server. By combining Outlook and Exchange, you can do things that Outlook cannot do on its own. With Exchange, users of Outlook can view a colleague's calendar, assign someone else the ability to respond to emails on that person's behalf, and do a whole host of other cool things right from their desktop.

It's hard for most Exchange users to realize that Microsoft Exchange Server is anything more than an extension of Outlook. In the end, it doesn't matter what the technical differences between Outlook and Exchange are; what matters is that Outlook and Exchange can handle a lot of tasks together that Outlook cannot.

Collaborating with Outlook's Help

Your company is probably like many others, where you spend a lot of time in meetings and even more time figuring out when to schedule meetings and agreeing on what to do when they are not scheduled. Meetings and decisions can be planned using Outlook. Even though some of these features are available to all Outlook users, Exchange users will get the most out of them.

Organizing a meeting

Suppose you want to meet with three colleagues. A meeting time is suggested by the first person. You then call the second person—only to discover that the second person isn't available at the time the first person wishes to meet. Then you and the second person agree on a time, only to find that the third person cannot attend.

With Outlook, you can view schedules, choose a date, and suggest a meeting time that everyone can agree upon with just one message.

You can invite several people to a meeting by following these steps:

- The Calendar can be accessed by clicking **the Navigation bar (or by pressing Ctrl+2)**.

- The Meetings tab of the Ribbon can be accessed by **pressing Ctrl+Shift+Q (or using the Home tab)**.
  A new meeting form will open.

- Select **the Scheduling Assistant button** in the Show group of the Meeting tab on the Ribbon.
  This displays the attendee availability page. Outlook won't display the Scheduling Assistant button if it isn't connected to an Exchange server. In this case, the button will be labeled "Scheduling."

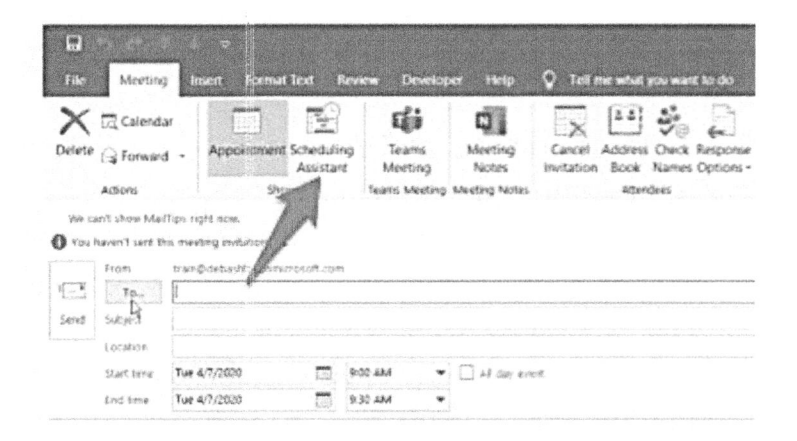

- To add participants, click the **"Add Attendees"** button at the bottom of the form.
   A dialog box will appear where you can choose attendees and resources.

- To invite someone to the meeting, simply **click on their name**.
   When you click on their name, it will be highlighted.

- Depending on how vital a person's participation is to the meeting, click the **"Required" or "Optional" button.**
   Based on the button you click, the name you select appears either in the Required or Optional box.

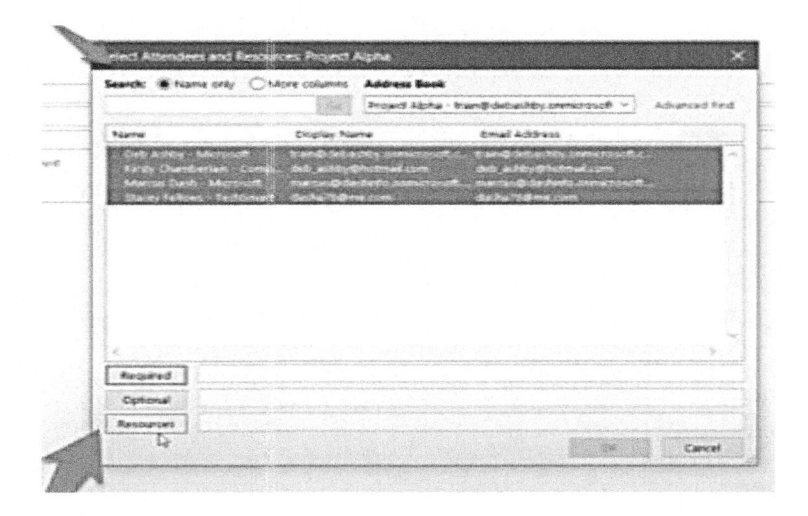

- Repetition **of steps 5 and 6** will help you choose whom to invite.
Select **attendees and resources**: The Global Address List displays your chosen names.

- You will see your selections on the Attendee Availability page once you click **OK.** In addition, if Outlook is connected to an Exchange server, the Attendee Availability page shows your team members' schedules so you can see when they have free time. Based on how it connects to the Exchange server, Outlook may not be able to get everyone's schedule right away. Outlook indicates it does not have information about participants' schedules if they do not connect with an Exchange server.

- You can choose the time that works best for you on the timeline at the top of the Attendee Availability page. Your chosen time appears in the Attendee Availability page's Start Time box. Instead of clicking the timeline, you can type the start time and end time of the meeting into the boxes at the bottom of the Attendee Availability page. The Suggested Times window provides a list of available times for everyone you're inviting to your meeting. If you don't see a time that works for everyone, you can pick a time from the list.

- Go **to the Meeting tab** and click **the Appointment button**. In the To section on the Appointment page, your invitees are listed.

- The "Subject" box should include the meeting's subject, while the "Location" box should include the location details.

- You can **enter meeting-related information** in the message box.

- Click the **"Send" button**.
  Upon submitting your meeting request, the people you invited will be notified, and you will be able to view the meeting in your calendar.

Responding to a meeting request

It's a possibility that you will be invited to a meeting, even if you don't organize them and send invitations, so it's a good idea to know how to respond to such an invitation.

The Meeting tab of the Ribbon displays these buttons when you've been invited to a meeting by email. You can access the drop-down menus for each of these buttons.

- **Accept:**

As soon as you decide to attend the meeting, Outlook adds it to your schedule and creates an email message to the person who organized it, telling them what you decided.

- **Tentative**

Your schedule is automatically updated with the meeting. The organizer receives an email message.

- **Make a New Time**:

You can suggest a different time if the meeting organizer picked an inconvenient one by clicking **"Propose New Time."**

You have two options:

- In the event that the original time cannot be accommodated, click **Decline** and then click **Propose New Time**.

- If you are unsure whether the original time will work and you want to suggest an alternate time, select **Tentative** and then click **Propose New Time**.

- Respond

Meeting invitations are sent to you via email, so you can click **"Respond"** to send a response to the email message without committing to the meeting in any way.

- **Calendar**

A separate Outlook window displays your complete calendar so you can see how your schedule looks.

If you want to add an explanation to the message, you can select **Edit the Response** Before Sending in the Accept, Tentative, or Decline buttons' menus, or choose Send the Response Now if you want to deliver the message right away.

In a meeting invitation, if the recipient is working with Exchange, a preview of their calendar is shown for the date and time of the meeting, giving them an overview of their availability. The preview represents only a small portion of the meeting's schedule and displays information about an hour or so before and after the meeting.

Checking responses to your meeting request

Every time you schedule a meeting in Outlook, you send a few emails inviting people to attend, and they respond immediately by either accepting or declining your invitation. Often, I need assistance in remembering who said "yes" and "no." It may be that you have a good memory. However, there is a feature in Outlook that keeps track of who says what.

Here are the steps you need to follow to check on the status of your meeting request:

- Go to **the navigation bar** and click **on Calendar**.
  You will see your calendar.

- Check the item by **clicking twice on it.**
  It opens.

- Choose the **"Tracking" button option**.
  Click the button itself, not the down arrow below it. To get where you need to be if you accidentally hit the down arrow, click **View Tracking Status**.
  You'll see the list of the people you invited and their responses.

Sadly, only the organizer of the meeting will know who has agreed to attend. To know whether you will meet that special someone you met in the elevator at a particular meeting, you will have to attend the meeting. When you get an email invitation to attend a meeting, you can check the participants' names via the mail.

Taking a vote

Teamwork and decision-making are constantly emphasized by management gurus. When most of the team members cannot be located most of the time, how can you get the team to make a decision? Take advantage of the voting buttons in Outlook to use it as a decision-making tool.

The voting feature of Outlook email lets you add buttons to emails sent to a group of people. Upon receiving the message, and if they are also using Outlook, recipients can respond by clicking a button. The responses in Outlook are automatically tallied, so you can track the office's momentum.

Following these steps while creating your email message will allow you to add voting buttons:

- You can create a new message by clicking **"New Email"** on the **Home tab of the Mail module**.
  This opens a message form.

- To use voting buttons, click **the Options tab on the Ribbon**. Select the buttons you want to use. Here are some suggestions:

    - Approve; Reject Yes; No Yes; No; Maybe

    - Custom

- The Properties dialog box appears if you choose Custom. Click the **"Use Voting Buttons"** and type your choices there. Just separate your choices with a semicolon according to the pattern suggested by the suggestions. For example, in order to allow people to vote on lunch menus, for example, list a range of options, such as pizza, hamburgers, and salads. Do not include spaces after the semicolons.

- Click **on the set of voting buttons** you want to use. A message indicating that you have added voting buttons appears at the top of your message. If you are adding your own custom choices, however, you will need to return to your message by clicking **the Close button** at the bottom of the Properties dialog box.

- Click on **the "Send" button**.

Tallying votes

Looking at the subject of a reply will show you who selected what when the replies arrive. A message from someone who chose to approve starts with the word "approve." A rejection message starts with the word "reject."

Check the Tracking tab on the message copy in your Sent Items folder for a full tally of your vote as well. Steps to do so are:

- Select **Sent Items** from the list of Folders.
  Your sent messages are displayed.

- **Click twice** on the message you sent for votes.
  It will open.

- Tracking can be accessed by clicking **the tracking button**. You see who voted and how they voted. An indicator shows the total number of votes cast.

Assigning tasks

It is always worthwhile to have someone else do something for you. A task can be assigned to another person, and then the progress of that person can be tracked.

You can assign a task to someone else by following these steps:

- Navigate **to Tasks** from the Navigation Bar.
  A list of tasks appears.

- Right-click **a task in the list of tasks.**
  You'll see a shortcut menu appear.

- The Assign Task option is available.
  A form is displayed.

- Just as with an email message, type the name of the person you are assigning the task to in the To field.
  This will appear in the To field.

- Click on **the "Send" button**.
  The task is now assigned to the individual you selected.

Your task recipient receives a message with two special buttons marked "Accept" and "Decline," similar to the meeting invitation I discussed earlier. As soon as the person accepts, the task is automatically added to their Outlook Tasklist, and if the person declines, the task will not be added to their task list.

Sending a status report

Assign Task is a feature that is extremely popular with people who give out tasks. It is less popular with people who have to do it. If you're more of a frequent task getter than a frequent task giver, look on the bright side, Outlook on an Exchange network can also keep your boss updated on your level of productivity.

On the task form, there are two boxes: status and percent complete. You can remind the top leadership of the value of your contributions by sending status reports if you keep the information in these boxes up-to-date.

Sending a status report is as simple as these steps:

- Go to **the navigation bar** and click **Tasks**.
  The task list appears.

- Click o**n any task twice**.
  A form for the task will appear.

- On the ribbon, click **Send Status Report**.
  There is a message window that appears, and the "To" box contains the name of whoever assigned the task.

- The text box at the bottom of the form is for any explanation you want to send about the task.
  Your text will appear on the form.

- Click **the "Send" button**.

Depending on your preference, you can send status reports on a weekly, daily, or hourly basis. Hopefully, leaving enough time between status reports will allow some tasks to be completed.

Collaborating with Outlook and Exchange

The features I describe in the rest of this chapter are not available to users of Outlook at home or without an Exchange server. It's not all bad news, however: Microsoft is working to make Exchange-only features available to all Outlook users, so you can use this section as a preview of what's to come.

Giving the delegate permission

Delegating authority is a skill that good managers possess. An assistant can sometimes be tasked with managing the boss's calendar, schedule, and even email if the boss is extremely busy. In this way, the boss is able to focus on what matters, while the assistant takes care of the details.

To name a delegate, follow these steps:

- In the left navigation pane, click **the Info button**, then click **the Account Settings button**.
  The Account Settings menu appears.

- Choose **Delegate Access from the menu**.
  A dialog box appears.

- Select **"Add" from the menu**.
  The Add Users dialog box appears.

- Identify each delegate by double-clicking **on his or her name**.
  You will see each name displayed in the Add Users window.

- To continue, click **OK**.
  In the Delegate Permissions dialog box, you can specify which permissions to give your delegate(s).

- The Delegate Permissions dialog box lets you make any changes you want.

- Once you click **OK**, the dialog box for Delegate Permissions closes. A list of the names you selected appears in Delegates.

- Click **OK** to close the Delegates dialog box.

Opening someone else's folder

Teams with close working relationships will often share calendars or task lists; not only can they see what each other is doing, but they can also enter appointments for team members—for example, if sales and service people work in the same office. In your role as a service person, you may find it useful if your sales partner is allowed to schedule appointments while you are out handling other clients.

Your partner will have to access your calendar in order to do this:

- In the left navigation pane, click **the Open & Export tab** on the File tab.

- Select **another user's folder from the menu.**
  A dialog box opens.

- Click on **the "Name" button**.
  A dialog box appears. (This is really the address book.)

- Open a person's folder by **clicking twice on his or her name**.
  Upon **closing the Select Name dialog box**, the name you **double-clicked appears** in the Open Other User's Folder dialog box.

- Click **the triangle** next to Folder Type.
  A list of folder types appears.

- You can view a folder by clicking **on its name**. A folder type box appears when you click **on a folder name**.

- When you click **OK**, you will be able to access the folder you selected, but where it is might not be obvious. By clicking **the Calendar button**, you can open the Folder pane so that you can see the other person's calendar. The calendar of the other person appears as a shared calendar in the Folder pane.

Viewing Two Calendars Side by Side

Executives often grant assistants access to their calendars. While the executive is doing something else, the assistant can keep the executive's schedule in order. Having both your boss's calendar and your own calendar displayed simultaneously can be useful when working as someone's assistant. You can view both calendars simultaneously in Outlook if you have the appropriate permissions (rights).

When you open the Folder pane after clicking the Calendar button and opening the calendar of someone else, you will see a section labeled "Shared Calendars." Once you have opened their calendar, the list of people you have Checking a name with the checkbox causes that person's calendar to appear directly beside yours. The date can be changed by clicking on the date you want to see, just as you would when viewing only one calendar.

It may be difficult to read your screen when you have two busy schedules side by side, so you might want to switch to a one-day view to keep it readable. Click the box next to the name of the other person in the Folder pane to return to viewing one schedule.

Setting access permissions

Sometimes, busy executives give their assistants full access to their Outlook accounts and even allow them to edit them right from their desks. With this strategy, the assistant organizes what the executive does, and the executive simply goes out and gets the job done. In this chapter, "giving delegate permissions" is described as granting access permissions, which is much like appointing a delegate.

To allow someone access to your account, you must grant them permission by following these steps:

- **Right-click** on the account name located in the Folders list in the Mail module.
  You will see your account name on top of the Inbox icon.
  Right-clicking an account name displays a shortcut menu.

- Permissions for a folder are selected.
  A Properties dialog box opens with the Permissions tab.

- Click **on the Add button**.
  A dialog box appears. (This is actually the Global Address list.)

- You can grant access to someone by **double-clicking** their name.
  A box appears at the bottom of the Add Users dialog box with the name that you **double-click**.

- Once you click **OK**, the Add User dialog box closes, and the name you selected appears in the Permissions dialog box's Name box.

- In the Properties dialog box, click **the name** you just added to the Name list.
It will be highlighted to indicate that it has been selected.

- To change permission levels, click **the triangle on the permission level box**.

- Select **a permission level from the list**.

   Permission levels confer a specific set of rights on the person who is assigned them. A reviewer, for instance, can only read items within your Outlook folders and can't add, edit, or remove them. The checkboxes next to the permission level boxes will tell you which rights you're granting. Those rights associated with each permission level will be marked with checkmarks.

- Having been granted permission to view your account as a whole, now you have to give permission to view each folder in the account individually. Almost every folder in Outlook can be made available to another person-even your Deleted Items and Junk Email folders if you like, but not your Contacts folder.

- You can let someone see a folder by right-clicking on it.
An option appears.

- Select **Permissions from the Properties menu**.

- **Steps 3–8 should be followed**.

   If you are granting access to another person, you can either follow these steps for each icon in the Folders list or read through the "Giving delegation permissions" section.

It is impossible to tell whether someone has given you permission to view their data unless you open one of their folders (or unless they tell you), which prevents nasty hackers from stealing several people's passwords at once.

Looking at two accounts

You can set up Outlook so that your own folders and your boss's folders appear together in your Outlook Folders list if your boss grants you permission to view his or her entire Outlook account.

You can add a second person's account to your Outlook view by following these steps:

- Select **your account name** from the Folders list by **right-clicking**.
  A menu appears when you right-click **on your account name**, located above the Inbox icon.

- Select **the Data File Properties option**.
  A dialog box showing the General tab appears.

- Select **the Advanced button**.
  A Microsoft Exchange dialog box appears.

- Select **the Advanced tab**.
  A dialog box for Microsoft Exchange opens.

- Select **the "Add" button**.
  A dialog box appears.

- The username of the person whose account you want to add should be typed in.

The username must be entered. There is no list of users to choose from in the dialog box. You will receive an error message if you do not type the username correctly or if the username you type does not exist. In this case, make sure your username is spelled correctly.

- To continue, click **OK.**
In the Mailboxes list on the Advanced tab of the Exchange dialog box, the user's name appears in the Add Mailbox dialog box.

- Click **OK** to close the Microsoft Exchange dialog box.

- Upon **clicking OK**, the dialog box for Data File Properties closes.

When you add someone else's account to Outlook, the folder pane shows the new person's items. In your Folders list, you'll notice a new section called "Mailbox," followed by the username of the new person; it's where the person's mail-related items are located, including the Inbox. In the Folder pane, select Calendar. The new calendar entry will appear in the My Calendar section, followed by the new user's username; this is where the new user's calendar can be found. So it goes for each module you are permitted to view by the person.

Managing Your Out of Office Message

If going on a vacation is one of the best parts of your job, constantly juggling work emails rather than drinking tropical drinks, you may find it difficult to enjoy your tropical vacation. By turning on the Out of Office message, you can notify all your valued colleagues of your absence. This way, Outlook will automatically reply to every email sent to you based on the information you provide.

Follow these steps to enable automatic replies:

- Select **the Automatic Replies** (Out of Office) option **under the File tab**.
  A new window will appear.

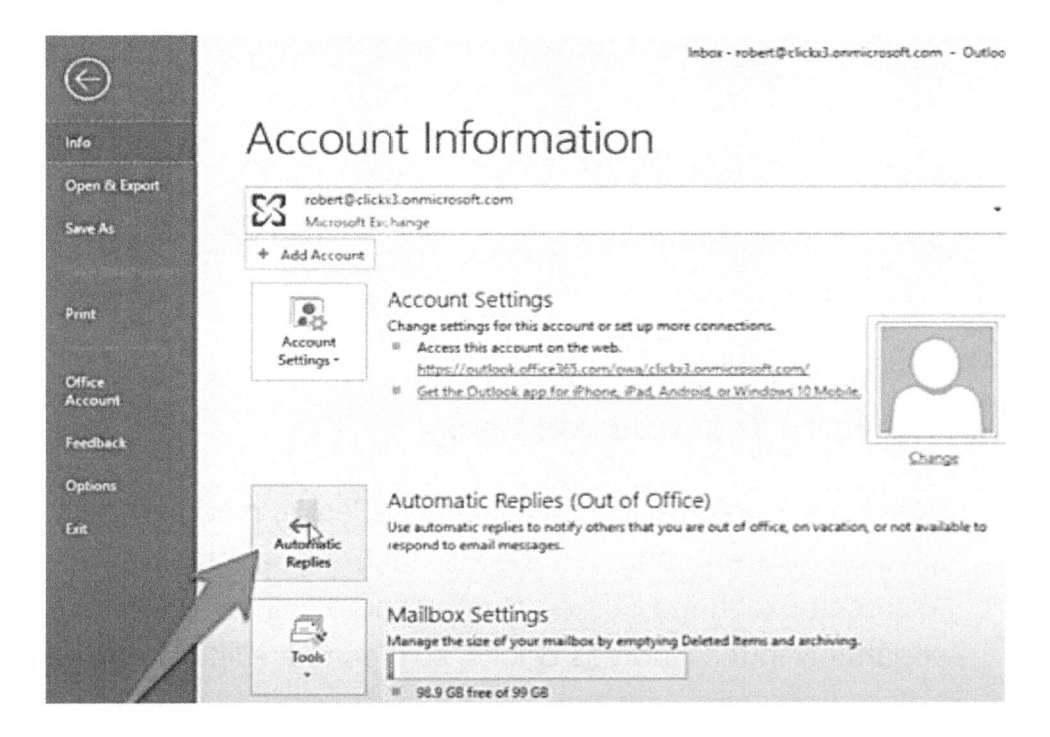

- Select **"Send Automatic Replies."**
  In the Automatic Replies dialog box, the gray text box at the bottom becomes white, as does the check box labeled "Only Send During This Time Period."

Basically, that tells you to enter a message that will be sent to all the people who email you while you're away. You may also specify the dates and times of your absence so that Outlook stops sending automatic replies after your scheduled absence has ended.

But this is optional. The purpose of an automatic reply is to send you a message, but leaving it blank defeats that purpose. You should fill in the blank with what you want to say.

- Then click **OK**.

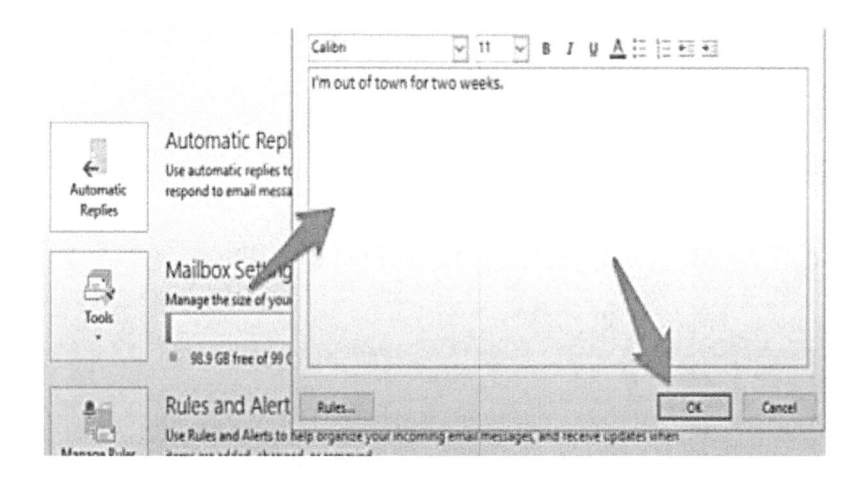

Managing Your Address Books

Besides your regular contact list in the People module, Outlook has several different address books that are actually part of the Microsoft Exchange Server. Names and email addresses are listed separately in the Address Books, so it can be a little confusing.

Contacts (what appear when you click on the People button in the Navigation bar) contain all sorts of personal data, while Address Books (what appear when you click the To button in a new message) contain only email addresses. You can also use an Address Book to send your messages to people on your corporate email system, especially if it is an Exchange Server system.

Let's take a look at your countless address books:

- **The Global Address List**

Outlook on corporate networks usually includes the names and email addresses of everyone in the company in the Global Address List that your system administrator maintains. With the Global Address List, you can send an email to anyone in your company without having to search for their email address.

- **The Address Book of Contacts**:

Email addresses in the Contacts Address Book are gathered from the Contacts list. Whenever you click the "To" button in Outlook, your contacts' address book will automatically be populated so you can quickly add people to an email.

- **Additional address books**:

When you create folders, you can also create separate address books for Outlook contacts. Additional address books can also be created by your system administrator.

Hopefully, you won't see your address book. In a global address list that someone else maintains, such as on a corporate network, all of the addresses of all the people you ever send email to are stored. In such a case, Outlook is perfect. Usually, you don't need to know what an address book is; you just enter the recipient's name in the To field of the message. The recipient's name will be checked for spelling, and Outlook will handle the rest for you. Your computer seems to have a tiny psychic inside who knows just what you need.

Occasionally, Outlook complains that it cannot send a message or can't determine to whom you're sending it. In this case, you have to enter the recipient's address. Outlook ignores addresses that are not in one of its address books or in a format Outlook understands. You need to either manually enter the complete address or add the recipient's name and address to your contacts list in these situations.

Scheduling a Skype Meeting

Some years ago, Microsoft purchased Skype, an online service that offers tools for conferencing, video chat, instant messaging, and various other types of collaboration. By slowly integrating Skype into Microsoft Office, the company is making it easier for employees who work remotely to collaborate.

You need to log into Skype first before you can use Skype meetings or set up Skype for Business on your computer. The Microsoft Office suite already contains the Skype for Business application. Most of the time, you will be able to sign in to Skype with your Windows credentials. However, if you cannot, contact your system administrator.

Setting up a Skype meeting

When you schedule a meeting through Outlook, you can use your Skype software as a virtual conference room. A Skype button is even available on the Meetings page. The invitation appears with a link, "Join Skype Meeting," if you click the button when setting up a meeting. Creating a Skype meeting is as easy as that.

Joining a Skype meeting

Skype meetings are easier to join than to create. Simply double-click on the appointment on your calendar when the meeting time arrives. You'll be automatically taken to the Skype program, and an audio conference will be established as soon as you click "Join

Skype Meeting." Skype also allows you to conduct video conferences via the internet. Once you hear people speaking, you can join the conversation. Once your conference is over, click the X in the upper-right corner of Skype.

CHAPTER 15

OUTLOOK FOR THE IPAD AND ANDROID PHONES

Microsoft's new slogan is "mobile-first". CEO Satya Nadella has pledged to make mobile computing a priority for the company. Sales of mobile devices have surged, while sales of traditional PCs are decreasing. Millions of people rely solely on their phones for all their computing needs.

For this reason, Microsoft Outlook is a welcome addition to mobile platforms. Although the products that are now called Outlook for Android and iPad originated from another company, they don't work the same as those on desktop Outlook. These are excellent products. Their differences from desktop Outlook are in many ways an improvement. Additionally, desktop Outlook's features and functions could never be crammed into a tiny smartphone screen, so these products reduce all features down to what's really important.

Understanding the Mobile Difference

According to a Pew Research Center study published in 2011, 35% of Americans owned smartphones. Since then, the figure has risen by nearly 77 percent. With that in mind, I think it's fair to say you have some experience with using a smartphone and how it differs from a laptop or desktop computer. A smartphone or tablet doesn't come with a keyboard; you work through everything by tapping the screen with your fingers. The process is similar to finger painting but without all the mess.

Using Mobile Email

When you're on the go and only have a phone to work with, it's important that you be able to perform useful tasks on your incoming email when you're away from your desk. Messages can be sorted, filed, and marked for later action with the help of mobile Outlook versions, which allows you to process your email more quickly and efficiently. Responding quickly to emails and letting people know you are available is easy with Outlook Mobile. Or perhaps so you look like you're working at your desk while you're actually away.

Reading email

If you use Outlook on your phone or tablet, you'll most likely read your email first. You can see a similar layout to the desktop version of Outlook on the iPad. The left pane shows a list of messages, and the right pane displays the contents of a message. The content of a message is displayed when you tap the message on the left of the list.

A mobile phone running Outlook will display only the message list. The message body can be seen by tapping the message in the message list. Simply swipe your finger across the message body from left to right to return to the message list. The back button on Android devices does the same thing as well.

Replying to email

You can respond to an email message almost as easily as you can read one. An icon with the appearance of a bent arrow appears at the bottom of the message. Click on it to see a menu of reply options, and then select your preferred option.

A message reply form opens. Choosing Reply All or Reply will automatically address the message to your intended recipients. Selecting Edit recipients allows you to add or remove recipients.

Composing an email

How convenient would it be if you could send an email while sitting in a park or in a cab? It is definitely more convenient than sitting at work.

Here are the steps to composing an email message in mobile Outlook:

- You can access the new email icon from the message list pane's top-right corner.

  That icon appears on an iPad as a square with a pencil in it. A circle with a plus sign appears in the lower-right corner of the Android screen. You see the New Message form, the on-screen keyboard, and a blinking cursor in the To field of the message form.

- Put the first few letters of the address or name of the person you are emailing.

  The moment Outlook sees a name or address beginning with the letters you type, it suggests matching names and email addresses. Chances are, the recipient is already listed. Simply tap on his or her name, and the name and address of that person will be automatically added to the To box. If the name doesn't appear, type in the email address completely.

- Enter **a subject in the Subject field**.
  Although a subject line isn't necessary, it is recommended.

- Enter **your message** in the main part of the message box.

- Click **the "Send" icon**. The message pane's upper-right corner displays the "Send" icon. It resembles an arrow pointing to the right. Touch it to send your message.

The steps for forwarding a message look very similar to those for composing a new message, except you have to enter an email address. Otherwise, there is no difference.

Archiving, scheduling, and deleting email messages

One thing that mobile Outlook offers you that is not available on desktop Outlook is the ability to swipe left or right on a message to quickly process it. The name of the thing you're about to do appears in a colored background as you slide messages right or left.

As soon as you install mobile Outlook, you are presented with two options: schedule and archive. There are several other options you can choose from, but you can only have two active at once: one for right-swiping and one for left-swiping.

Other options include:

- **Schedule**:

If you swipe right to schedule a message, it will be hidden until you choose to show it again. You can choose from a range of options when scheduling a message, from a few hours out to tomorrow. It is also possible to specify a time.

- **Delete**:

As it says, it's over with a tap. Your mail server might allow you to retrieve it from the trash.

- **Archive:**

You can choose this option to direct the message to a particular folder that you've chosen beforehand. You must have selected an archive folder for this to work, or else it will not work. Thankfully, it offers to set up an archive folder if you have not already done so. From then on, all your archiving goes into that folder.

- **Move:**

With this option, the message is moved to a folder, but you are asked to choose which one every time.

- **Mark Flagged:**

This will flag the message so you'll remember to go back to it just like you do on your desktop.

- **Mark Read:**

Each message in Outlook is marked as read once it has been read. There may be times when you want to mark things as read without actually reading them. This is a convenient way to do it.

- **Mark Read and the Archive:**

This combines the two previous choices under the same name.

- **No Action**

Is it worth it? It doesn't make any difference.

The swipe feature will still be useful even when these settings are left in their original state-Schedule and Archive. Consider, however, which options may work best for you based on how often you use email.

You can change the swiping options by following these steps:

- Tap on **the action menu button** (three horizontal lines) in the upper-left corner to launch a menu.
It is sometimes called the "hamburger button" because the three horizontal lines are similar to those on a hamburger.

- Go **to Settings (the gear icon).**
You will see the Settings menu.

- Swipe through the available options.
A screen will appear with swipe options. Sliding your finger down the menu a bit may be necessary.

- Swipe Right or Swipe Left anywhere in the Swipe Right or Swipe Left areas.
This brings up the menu of options previously listed.

Select your preferred option.

- Return to **the settings page** by tapping the Back arrow at the top of the screen.

- The Settings screen can be closed by tapping **the Close (X) button** in the upper-left corner.

Deleting messages

The easiest thing you can do in mobile Outlook is deleting a message. A trash can-shaped icon appears at the top of the message screen. Simply tap it and your message will be sent there. The trash can will not appear if there is no message selected. According to your mail server and Outlook settings, the trash can may be automatically emptied at a certain interval, or you may have to empty the trash yourself.

Managing groups of messages

You can process and read emails much more easily with Mobile Outlook than you can send them. It is still better to compose an email on a desktop or laptop. Although it offers a clever way to handle multiple messages at once, Open the message list and hold your finger on the message you want to check. Check the box next to each message you want to process, and the box will be marked. You can delete all the messages you checked by tapping the trash can icon now.

The flag icon flags them all. You can also select other options such as moving or marking unread messages from the three-dot menu in the top-right corner of the message list on a phone.

Using Your Mobile Calendar

There is also a slick version of the calendar that you see in the desktop version of Outlook on mobile devices. various features, but just those that are most likely to be used and work well on a phone or tablet. Access the calendar by tapping the calendar button below. If you see the message "No Connected Calendars" on this device, you can't use the Outlook Calendar feature for the email account you are using. It is possible to create an additional account that does include a calendar, or you can simply use the calendar feature on iOS or Android.

Navigating the mobile calendar

On a computer screen, calendars occupy a huge amount of space; think about a month's worth of appointments. Mobile devices have such small screens that this can be a problem. Depending on the size of the device, mobile Outlook displays your calendar differently: a tablet displays your calendar one way, a phone another.

The two calendars must therefore be managed differently. If you are using an iPad, you can get to the calendar by tapping on the calendar icon at the bottom of the screen. If you are using a phone, you need to tap the hamburger button, also known as the three-line menu, in the top-left corner, and then tap Calendar.

Similarly, a tablet can show you a full, hour-by-hour view of the entire workweek, whereas a phone can only show you an hour-by-hour view of a single day. Regardless, you can swipe the calendar to see days that come before or after the day you have selected.

Creating a new appointment

A plus sign appears in the upper-right corner of the screen on both versions of the mobile Outlook Calendar. To open a new event, tap the plus sign. The settings for each line of text on the appointment form can be accessed by tapping on the line. In the form, you can adjust the date, time, location, and more.

You should choose desktop Outlook over mobile Outlook if you create a lot of appointments. The mobile Outlook app offers you a convenient way to view your calendar while out and about, but it also makes it hard to handle details on a mobile device, where you can only use taps and swipes. You'll see that entering an appointment in desktop Outlook is much faster than entering one in mobile Outlook. Nevertheless, mobile apps are updated on an almost monthly basis, so chances are it will be much simpler by the time you read this.

CHAPTER 16

TELECOMMUTING WITH OUTLOOK.COM AND THE OUTLOOK WEB APP

We're going virtual! According to experts, the number of people working from virtual offices for virtual companies is expected to increase in the near future.

Our brave new world would not be possible without the Internet. Even though Outlook works great on the web, sometimes it might not be feasible to carry around a full-blown version of it wherever you go, and you may need a little more power than a mobile version provides. However, you can access all of your emails in Outlook.com or Hotmail.com, as well as your contacts and calendar, from any web-connected computer by using Outlook.com. You can improve your results when you use Outlook.com.

Signing In to Outlook.com

The Outlook web-based email service from Microsoft is completely free. The service is somewhat similar to Google's Gmail, but it has a twist: it connects directly to desktop Outlook data. As part of the merge, Microsoft has combined Hotmail and Windows Live into a single email service. The service also now supports Facebook, Twitter, and LinkedIn contacts, as well as your calendar.

A Microsoft account is required to access Outlook.com. It's likely that you have an account that you use to sign in to Windows, for example, OneDrive or Xbox Live. You can use other email addresses at Outlook.com once you've signed in to your Microsoft account.

When you first visit Outlook.com, you'll be taken to a sign-in screen. Create a free account or sign in using your Microsoft account.

Signing into Outlook.com for the first time may display several setup screens. In addition to your language and time zone, you might also have to enter a theme color, a default signature, and your phone number. Click through the setup process to the end, entering any of those details as you wish.

Exploring the Outlook.com Interface

In terms of function, Outlook.com is identical to the desktop version of Outlook, so you won't need to learn any new tricks or techniques, but its visual appearance may differ from the desktop version.

The Outlook.com interface is available in two versions. You can enjoy ad-free, enhanced Outlook.com with an Office 365 subscription. You get a similar experience if you have a free Microsoft account, but with an advertisement on the right side of the screen.

These are some of the notable features.

There are six folders by default on the left side of the screen: Inbox, Junk Email, Drafts, Sent Items, Deleted Items, and Archive.

- To access the other modules in Outlook.com, you use the navigation buttons along the far left side of the screen. Additionally, there are four other modules: Calendar, People, Photos, and Tasks. (Note that Outlook.com does not have a notes module.)

- At the top of the screen, there is a toolbar in place of the ribbon. The commands on the toolbar vary depending on what you're selecting.

- **You can choose from the following icons in the upper-right corner (from left to right):**

    - **Skype:** Begin a new Skype conversation

    - **Manage Premium:** This feature is only available if you have an Office 365 subscription, which opens a window that lets you work with premium-only tools and view your storage usage.

    - **Settings:** This allows you to customize some common settings, including themes, conversation views, sorting, grouping, and the reading pane.

    - **What's New:** It displays information about how to use the latest features.

    - **Help:** Displays a help screen for Outlook.com.

    - **Account:** Makes it easy to edit your profile, check your account status, or log out.

Getting Caught Up on Web Email Basics

Outlook.com lets you access your inbox from any browser, so you can read office gossip or delete spam from Nigerian oil magnates.

Reading messages

You can access Outlook.com from any computer with an internet connection since it is webmail. It is possible to access your Hotmail, Messenger, and Outlook.com mail. Most people use the Inbox as a to-do list, and Outlook.com enables this from any computer with an Internet connection.

Here are the steps for reading your messages:

- Navigate **to the Inbox folder**.
  You will see your messages there.

- Click **on the message you'd like to read**.
  The message text is displayed in the reading pane on the right side of the screen. When you click on the message name in the message list, the content appears in the reading pane.

Sending a message

Whenever you want to shoot off a quick email from your favorite Internet cafe, you can do so with Outlook.com in a flash. Your message will be ready before you know it.

The next step is to do the following:

- On the Folders page, click Inbox.
  The messages you have in your inbox will appear.

- Navigate to the Ribbon and click New Message.
  A window opens.

- Complete the New Message screen.
  Your recipient's address goes in the "To" box, your subject

goes in the "Subject" box, and your message goes in the "main field."

- On the Ribbon, click the Send button.
Now your message will be sent out.

Choosing the message's importance

When composing a message using Outlook.com, you can select a priority between "High," "Normal, and "Low." Select the Set Importance option from the drop-down menu by clicking the **More button** above the message composition pane.

Flagging messages

Messages can be flagged to give them extra attention. In your inbox, flagged messages will show at the top. There are no levels, and there is no dated reminder feature (like in the desktop version). If you would like to flag a message, select it and then, on the toolbar above the message, click the **More button**. The Flag menu will appear.

Organizing Contacts

Having access to your collection of information from anywhere is the whole point of Outlook.com, and keeping track of your contact list is essential.

Viewing the contacts

You can change the appearance of contacts by clicking the Filter icon in the upper-right corner of the Contacts list pane. Then you can choose your preferences.

Adding contacts

The Contacts list in Outlook.com can be updated from anywhere. For instance, if you attend a conference or convention and exchange business cards with many people, you should add their names right away to your contacts list.

It doesn't matter what your device is (whether it's a laptop, tablet, or smartphone), you can access your account remotely to add those new addresses before you leave where you are.

Using Outlook.com, you can add a new contact by following these steps:

- To create a new contact, click **the New Contact button** in the upper-left corner of the People module.
  A form will appear.

- Complete **the New Contact form**.

- Then click **Save**.
  As soon as the form closes, the name you entered in the New Contact box appears in your Contacts list.

You can edit a contact record by opening the record, clicking the **Edit button** on the Ribbon, and following the same steps.

Using Your Calendar

Outlook.com's calendar design is constantly improving thanks to Microsoft. In other words, what you see today might not be what you see in a few weeks, although the features might not change. For this reason, Web-based applications are both wonderful and annoying.

Viewing your calendar

Experts suggest managing your schedule for the long term, medium term, and short term. In Outlook.com, you can view your appointments in several ways, depending on what you want (or don't want) to see.

The View drop-down menu will be visible in the upper-right corner of the screen. This could be referred to as a day, a week, etc., depending on the current view.

Select the view you wish to use:

- Day shows the day's appointments.
- A week shows a week.
- The workweek corresponds to Monday through Friday.
- A month shows a month.

Outlook.com does not show your schedule details, but you can add and edit items so that you can see the big picture and then deal with the details at your desk.

Entering an appointment

Those who travel extensively probably keep their calendar on a smartphone, but the majority of people use Outlook calendars to manage their meetings and appointments. Since Outlook.com is linked to your Outlook appointments and meetings, you can check where you need to be and with whom from any Internet-capable device. From now on, you'll be able to plan meetings and lunches.

To enter an appointment, follow these steps:

- In the bottom-left corner of the screen, click **the Calendar button** to switch to **the Calendar module**. Your appointments will appear on the calendar.

- In the left-hand corner of the screen, click **the New Event button**.
  You are prompted to create an appointment.

- Add a title by clicking on **the "Add a Title"** placeholder. Put something about your appointment, like meeting Bambi and Godzilla.

- Enter the **location** of your appointment in the Location box. Maybe central Tokyo? Or maybe the pediatrician's office?

- A calendar name appears in the top bar of the pop-up window (such as My Calendar). Select **the right calendar** from the drop-down menu if you have more than one. Outlook.com supports multiple calendars.

- Click on the **Start date and choose the start date**. The date might not be displayed in the pop-up calendar, so click the arrows next to the month name to see the date.

- Select **a start time for your appointmen**t by clicking **the down arrow** on the first time box.

- Select **the end time in the second time box** by clicking **the down arrow**.

- The recurrence (repeat) and reminder options can be selected as desired.

- Then click **Save**.
  Your Outlook.com Calendar will notify you by email when you have upcoming appointments each day. Simply click **on the link to view the details**.

Moving to an appointment

You can move an appointment to a new time and date by simply dragging it.

Changes other than the date and time of your appointment can be made by following these steps:

- Click twice **on the appointment.**

- Choose **the information** you want to change.

- Update your information.

- Then click **Save**.
  You can delete an appointment by selecting **it and clicking Delete on the toolbar**.

Exploring Your Options

The options in Outlook.com can be adjusted to a limited extent. Click **the Settings button** (it looks like a gear) in the upper-right corner of your screen to access the options.

Options can be set at two levels. When you click **on the Settings button**, a list of the most common and basic ones appears. The options vary according to the module.

To see more options Click **View Full Settings at the bottom** of the task pane, which opens the Settings dialog box. On the left side of the navigation pane, you can switch between the options for different modules the same way you can do it in the Outlook Settings dialog box.

Automated vacation replies or out of office messages

In the desktop version of Outlook, you can set an "Out of Office" message to notify coworkers when you're out of the office (or simply unavailable). Outlook.com has a similar tool called the Automated Vacation Response. It's an easy and fun way to tell everyone you're on vacation.

All you need to do is:

- At the top of the Outlook.com Mail screen, click **the Settings icon**.

- At the bottom of the pane, click **the "View Full Settings" button**.
  A dialog box appears.

- Go to the middle pane and click **"Automatic Replies."** An automatic reply settings window will appear.

- Enable automatic replies by clicking the **"Automatic Replies On" control.**

- If you choose the **"Send Replies Only During a Time Period"** checkbox, please enter the **start and end dates and times**.

- Fill out **the Out-of-the-Office Message placeholder** by clicking the **"Add a Message Here"** button.

- **Save** your changes.

- Click **the Close (X) button**.

Don't feel guilty about disregarding those emails anymore. When you get back to the office, remember to turn off auto-replies. If not, everyone will think you are still having fun.

Creating a signature

Outlook.com allows you to create only one signature, which you can include when you want. You might use a very grand and formal signature for business-not only to impress lackeys and sycophants, but also to intimidate enemies. Unless, of course, you only have lackeys and sycophants as friends, in which case you should leave it off your messages. You certainly should go heavy on the praise, Your Royal Highness!

Following these steps will allow you to add a signature to Outlook.com:

- At the top of Outlook.com Mail, click **the Settings icon**.

- Click **View Full Settings** at the bottom of the pane.
  A dialog box appears.

- Select **Compose and Reply** from the middle pane.
  A box appears for the signature.

- Fill in the signature field with your text.
  Format your text as desired using the tools above the box.

- You can now click **"Save."**
  The Settings dialog box is closed.

Understanding the Outlook Web App

As part of Microsoft Exchange, the Outlook Web App facilitates advanced features of Outlook, such as public folders, shared calendars, and assigned tasks. Many big and small companies run exchanges for this purpose. Many companies that operate on Microsoft Exchange do not offer Outlook Web Apps. If your company does, however, you can access Outlook from anywhere you have a computer: a public library, an Internet cafe, or even the local photocopy shop. A web app is not difficult; the Outlook Web App is a special website that looks and behaves quite a bit like the desktop version of Outlook. It is possible that the Outlook Web App will look different if your organization is using an older version of Microsoft Exchange. However, the fundamental features should remain the same.

Knowing when it's handy

Despite the fact that the Outlook Web App is much more powerful than the desktop version of Outlook, you may find it incredibly convenient to access your Outlook data if you find yourself in the following circumstances:

- Taking a laptop with you on a very short business trip just to check your email may not be practical.

- In cases where you need to work from home from time to time, but don't want to spend time setting up your home computer to connect to the office network,

- Whenever you want to do some simple planning and collaborate with your coworkers, use someone else's computer.

- If you're getting an email on your smartphone (including an iPhone, Android, or another smart device) and want to send a more detailed response than you can with the tiny keyboard,

Signing in and out

Open a browser, enter the address of the page that your company has set up for accepting logins to the Outlook Web App, and then enter your username and password as you would on any other website. Depending on your organization, the process may differ slightly. Ask your system administrator for details.

Using the Outlook Web App is as easy as surfing the Internet. It does not require any special equipment. All you need is your username and password, as well as the address of your Outlook Web App page.

CHAPTER 17

TEN SHORTCUTS WORTH TAKING

The following tips will help you boost your productivity, including turning a message into a meeting and resending it. You can boost your Outlook productivity with these ten accessories, including Skype, OneDrive, and an online service for backing up your data.

Also learn why you cannot have a unified inbox in Outlook as well as how you cannot create a distribution list from an email.

Using the New Items Tool

In whatever module you are in, click the tool on the far-left side of the ribbon to add a new item.

So you change the name and appearance of this icon when you change modules, so it becomes the New Task icon when you switch to the Task module, the New Contact icon when you switch to the People module, and so forth.

Alternatively, you can click **the New Items tool** just to the right of it to access the menu.

New Items allows you to create a new item in a module other than the one you're in without switching modules.

You might want to create a task while you're answering an email. Choose Task from the list of new items, create your task, then continue working with your email.

Sending a File to an Email Recipient

Using Outlook email, you can send a file with just a few mouse clicks, regardless of whether Outlook is running.

If you're using File Explorer to view your files, you can mark any file for sending to any recipient.**Here's what you need to do:**

- Use File Explorer **to locate the file**.

- To send a file, **right-click on it**.

- You are presented with a menu.

- Choose **the recipient**.

- A new menu appears.

- Select **the recipient of the mail**.

- There is a form for new messages.

- The attached file is represented by an icon in the attached box.

- Include the subject of the file and the email address of the person you're sending it to.

- Adding a comment to your message is as simple as typing it in the message area.

- Click the **"Send" button**.

- The message is delivered to the receiver.

Sending a File From a Microsoft Office Application

Office documents can be emailed directly from the application itself without using Outlook.

Follow the steps below to achieve that:

- Click **the File tab** while an Office document is open in the application that created it.

- Select Shares

- You will see the share dialog box.

- Under Attach a Copy Instead, choose **Word Document or PDF**.

- Depending on the share, choose **whichever format is most appropriate**.

- Choose Word if you want the recipient to be able to edit the document easily, and PDF if that is not what you want.

- Outlook shows a new message form.

- Send **the file to the recipient's email address**. The subject of the file should be the person's name and email address.

- Under **the icon for the file**, there is a text box where comments can be entered.

- Click on **the "Send" button**.

- The Outbox receives your message.

Turning a Message Into a Meeting

Occasionally, after exchanging dozens of email messages about a topic, it would be faster to talk. Creating a meeting from an email message is as easy as **clicking the Meeting button** on the Home tab (in the Inbox with the appropriate

You can then create a meeting based on the contents of the email by clicking on the New Meeting button.

Finding Something

You can accumulate a lot of items in Outlook in no time, which can then take a while to search through when you are looking for one specific item.

Outlook can help you find items quickly if you type the name of the item in the search field at the top. That launches a quick search, so you can find what you are looking for in no time.

Undoing Your Mistakes

It's time you learned about the Undo command if you didn't already. The Ctrl+Z shortcut key can be used to undo accidentally entered text, as can the Undo button in the upper left corner of the screen in the Quick Access Toolbar.

You can experiment without worrying about the consequences; the worst thing you can do is undo it! It is best if you go back and fix your mistake right away before doing so many things.

Using the "Go to Date" Dialog Box

Any calendar view can be accessed using the "Go to Date" dialog box. You'll find it under the "Go-To" group on the Home tab, under Properties. You can also use Ctrl+G as a shortcut.

Adding Items to List Views

You can add an item to a list at the top of most Outlook lists by typing something into the blank field. Simply click **the "Add a New Task"** button to begin.

Your new item will be entered into the field once you click **on it**.

Sending Repeat Messages

Since you might send out one or two messages repeatedly, store them as Quick Parts to save time.

The steps you should follow when finding an Outlook accessory vendor online are:

- Your email message should be addressed.
- The email address of the company appears in my browser.
- Select **the Insert tab**.
- Click **the Quick Parts button** in the message body.
- Your saved AutoText item will appear.
- Make **certain changes to reflect the name of the product.**
- Click on **the "Send" button**.

Your request can be sent in less than 30 seconds and you can then move on to the next task.

Using this feature requires you to first store text blocks in Quick Parts:

- Choose **the text** you want to repeat in an email message, appointment, contact record, meeting, or task.

- Select **the Insert tab**.

- To access Quick Parts, click **the Text group** button.

- Select **"Save Selection to Quick Part Gallery."**

You can organize Quick Part text into groups according to their purpose. You could, for instance, generate the text for introductory messages and closing messages for different types of messages and then store them.

Resending a Message

When someone forgets to do something you asked them to do, sometimes you need to remind them.

A new message could be written, telling that person how often you've reminded him or her already.

However, this is quicker and easier:

- Open **your Sent Items folder**.

- Go back **to the message you sent last time** and click **it twice**.

- Decide what action to take.

- You can resend this message by choosing **this option**.

- Additionally, you could add the following: "Here is another copy in case you didn't receive the first."

CHAPTER 18

TEN ACCESSORIES FOR OUTLOOK

Although Outlook can do a lot by itself, a few thoughtful accessories can make things even easier. Many of my favorite accessories compensate for many of the features Outlook is missing. I also use some of my favorite accessories to access my Outlook data wherever I am.

Smartphones

Smartphones are ubiquitous today, and they are probably Outlook's most powerful accessory.

A smartphone is a cell phone with an integrated personal organizer. If you haven't looked for a new cell phone lately, you should.

Smartphones based on Android and the iPhone are right now the top choices.

Despite the ease with which I can enter and manage data with Outlook, I always have my most important Outlook information with me on my smartphone.

My smartphone even allows me to read my email on the subway (an experience I wouldn't have with a laptop).

A Tablet Computer

The tablet is rapidly becoming an important part of many people's lives. While the Apple iPad is the most well-known and most popular tablet, there are several Android tablets on the market as well. I have an older iPad 2, and it is perfectly sufficient to run Outlook on the go.

The larger screen of a tablet makes reading email more comfortable, which is an advantage for people who receive dozens of emails each day.

Meanwhile, a tablet's lightweight and convenient size allow you to easily scan your email anywhere you are, from coffee shops to restaurants to limos.

E-Learning

With computers, everything changes so rapidly, it's almost impossible to stay current.

It is imperative to keep learning constantly, but how can one find instruction? Search online for resources such as this book you are reading. You can also visit Youtube to watch video clips.

Whether you want to become proficient in Microsoft Office, social media, or even such impressive subjects as calculus, you can learn at your own pace. By spending enough time on the internet, you can become incredibly smart.

Microsoft Office

The first version of Outlook was included in the Microsoft Office 97 suite.

Microsoft offers Outlook as a stand-alone product in some cases (or in conjunction with Internet Explorer), so you may not always enjoy all the benefits of using Microsoft Office and Outlook in concert.

It's easy to send outgoing emails and graphics with Office, while Outlook makes it simple to share your work via the web and email. I would advise using both if need be.

A Business-Card Scanner

With business card scanners, the information on business cards you collect at meetings, trade shows, and conferences can be copied into Outlook with ease. While you can enter all the information manually, using a business card scanner can save you lots of time if you collect more than a few dozen cards per week.

Online Backup

You can choose from several good online backup services at an affordable price, including Mozy and Carbonite.

You can restore your information if your computer crashes or if you suffer a fire, flood, or another disaster that destroys your computer. In order to use any of these services, you will need a fast Internet connection. Their monthly fee is worth every penny, and the peace of mind is priceless.

Skype

Skype can be used to host the online meetings you're likely to plan in your Outlook Calendar using an easy-to-maintain virtual conference service.

There's even a button on the ribbon that you can tap to launch a Skype meeting (if you're using Office 365 for business).

If you often meet with colleagues who work from home or from different locations, Skype can make your life a whole lot easier.

Microsoft SharePoint

Microsoft SharePoint was most commonly used in large organizations that needed ways of sharing information and collaborating smoothly.

Private users and home businesses found the program too complicated and expensive.

In today's world, anyone can subscribe to Office 365 and thereby obtain SharePoint. The price depends on how much service you want and what level of service you want.

You may want to investigate SharePoint as a tool for sharing documents and other information if you regularly collaborate on business projects with a team.

Microsoft Exchange

There are many business-oriented features in Outlook that require a program called Microsoft Exchange to function, such as shared calendaring.

The Exchange server allows you to share Outlook data and office tasks with others in your organization.

In Office 365, you can rent Microsoft Exchange accounts. Fees vary depending on the number of optional features you select and the size of the workforce in your company.

OneDrive

File sharing is made easier with OneDrive, a service from Microsoft.

As long as you have a Microsoft account, you have a OneDrive account; both accounts are connected. Sign in to onedrive.com using your Microsoft ID to access the service. The OneDrive icon in the navigation pane of Windows 10 also gives you access to OneDrive.

If you have OneDrive's settings checked, you can determine which files and folders are cached locally, so you can use them even when you are not online. (To access OneDrive's settings, you must right-click on the icon on the taskbar and choose Settings.)

CHAPTER 19

TEN THINGS YOU CAN'T DO WITH OUTLOOK

When you first get Outlook, it won't be able to do any of these ten things.

The geeky programmers tell me you can reprogram Outlook to accomplish many of these tasks using Visual Basic shortcut macros.

In addition to being outside the scope of this book, it's also something that normal, sensible people would not do.

Create a Unified Inbox

There is nothing unusual about having multiple email accounts. People often separate their business and personal accounts.

Most people today use email on two or more devices at once, typically a personal computer and a mobile phone. If you use IMAP, the kind of email made for sending across multiple devices, you can't create a unified inbox on your desktop.

The iPad and Android versions of Outlook offer unified inboxes but not the large desktop client. It would be very useful if it happened, but it doesn't in this version.

Adding a Phone Number to Your Calendar

If Outlook could be configured to automatically look up the phone number of the person you're meeting and insert that number into an appointment record, that would be perfect.

Outlook does not have an address lookup feature like many smartphones. Perhaps another time.

Open a Message From the Reading Pane

Many people use Outlook to keep a record of everything they do and everything they send and receive.

From time to time, you may scroll through your messages again and again to keep track of who you've spoken to and when.

In a very long list, if you select one message to be displayed in the Reading pane and then scroll through the list, you cannot right-click on the Reading pane to open the message you're viewing.

Right-clicking the message in the Reading pane doesn't seem to be too difficult for Microsoft; however, it isn't included.

Performing Two-sided Printing

Printing out your schedule and keeping it in a binder makes it look exactly like a timetable in an old-fashioned planner.

Outlook does not understand how to reorganize printed pages in accordance with whether you view the page on the left side or the right side of the book when you print it.

If this is an extremely minor quibble, but if it's important to you, you'll have to accept one-sided printing.

Searching and Replacing Area Codes

Outlook cannot automatically change all 312s to 708s; you must do that individually.

There is a Microsoft utility for changing Russian area codes, but not for changing area codes in the United States!

Printing a List of Meeting Attendees

While preparing for a large meeting organized using Outlook, especially a conference call, it's handy to maintain a list of attendees.

It is possible to keep the meeting item open on your calendar, but you cannot do that if you are presenting at the same time.

Enlarging the Type in the Calendar Location Box

Today, most conference calls are organized in Outlook, and participants can browse the location box on the calendar form to enter their dial-in numbers.

In a hurry after finishing your last conference call, those teeny-weeny numbers are tough to discern, especially when your eyes aren't as sharp as hawks. My recommendation is to use a magnifying glass.

Creating Contact Records for All Email Recipients

If an email is sent to a large number of people, you can create a distribution list from it by copying them all to a group.

Dragging a message from one person to the People icon will also create a new contact record for that person.

To create contact records for a group of people, you must create a record for each individual—no dragging and dropping or copying and pasting is allowed.

Tracking Meeting Time Zones

In many cases, Outlook is used to coordinate Skype meetings and conference calls among people in different time zones.

In the past, I've often had to schedule phone calls between London, Sydney, and my home in New York.

Using the scheduling tool in Outlook Calendar, users are able to see each other's working hours-if they've set them up but it does not display what time of day it is where they are located.

When arranging a meeting whose timing happens to be awful for someone, it's helpful to know just how awful it will be.

Then, you'll be able to make it a bit less awful.

While there are websites that help you understand the time in various time zones, they do not provide availability information like the one you get in Outlook.

It is therefore imperative to make one guess at a time and to apologize when you make the wrong one.

Easily Backup Outlook Data

Although Outlook has been in the market for over 20 years, it has never been given an adequate means of keeping its data safe.

It's well known that you should always back up all the data on your computer, and you can make copies of your critical Outlook data (some of those tiny memory keys can do the trick, and you can download Outlook data to a handheld computer if necessary), but it's odd that no such feature has ever been added to Outlook itself.

You can stay safe if you get your email service from Microsoft Office 365, which stores all Outlook data safely in the cloud.

CHAPTER 20

TEN THINGS YOU CAN DO AFTER YOU'RE COMFORTABLE

Take Notes

You can easily type a quick note in Outlook's Notes module, and then go on with what you were doing. Ctrl+Shift+N opens a note, you type some text, and then you press **Esc** to close it.

In the Notes module,

- Click **the Notes tab** to open the full list of notes.
- To read a specific note, **double-click the notes tab button**.

As a feature, it dates from Outlook's early days, when it emerged from the primordial ooze.

Customizing the Quick Access Toolbar

With Office 2019/Office 365, there are no menus and instead a ribbon, tabs, and button arrangement of controls.

Though it is an excellent way to get a variety of commands into a small space, I sometimes have trouble understanding how to do many of the tasks I would like to accomplish.

When I find the command I need, I'm often unable to remember how I got there when I need to use it again. It's not all doom and gloom. After you've located the tool you need, you can right-click it and choose to add it to the quick access toolbar.

In that way, a tiny icon is added to that thin strip of icons that sits just above the Ribbon. The Quick Access Toolbar is kind of like a bookmark bar for the commands you want to keep track of, just as you would bookmark websites in your web browser to return to them later.

Every form in Outlook has its own Quick Access Toolbar, which is customized separately from the others. This is useful if you perform some tasks frequently using certain forms only. If you like to print individual email messages from time to time, for example, you can add the Quick Print command when you're reading or composing a message.

Wising Up Your Messages with Smart Art

Designs have the power to make any person look smart if they know what they're doing.

Smart Art is another intriguing feature on the Ribbon's Insert tab that you can use if you don't know what you're doing. With Smart Art, you can add colorful, annotated infographics to your emails.

Follow these steps to learn more about Smart Art:

- Open a new message composition window and click **the Insert tab**.

- Select **the SmartArt button**.

- Get a feel for a few designs.

Your Email Messages Should Be Translated

Perhaps your incoming emails are written in a foreign language if they seem so unclear.

You can translate incoming email messages in Outlook this way:

- Select **some foreign-language text in a message**.

- Simply **right-click the selection**.

- An options menu appears.

- Select **"Translate."**

- If you prefer, you can click **the Translate button** on the Review tab on the Ribbon of the message window.

- The research task pane will be displayed.

- Choose **the From and To languages from the menu** that is displayed in the task pane.

- Go **through the translation** in the lower part of the task pane.

If you cannot make sense of what has been translated, you will then know it is not your fault as you have tried your best.

Including Impact Charts

A chart tool is located just beneath the SmartArt button on the Insert tab of the Ribbon.

Your email will appear positively ordered once you use this tool (regardless of how disordered your mind may be).

Chart it up with these steps:

- Choose **the chart tool** under the Insert tab of your new email message.

- The chart gallery has two parts: a list of general chart types on the left and examples of each type on the right.

- The left side of the page offers a list of general types.

- On the right, you can select **a specific type**.

- Select **OK**.

In Email, Use Symbols

To add symbols, such as the euro currency symbol, to your email messages,

- Simply click **the Symbol button** on the Insert tab while writing an email message

- Select **the symbol you want**.

If you choose more symbols, you can also insert such clever things as fractions, arrows, and strange hieroglyphics to baffle your recipients into complying with your wishes.

Opening a number of calendars

You can create more than one calendar in Outlook. You might want to do so to track the activities of more than one person or to keep your business life separate from your personal life (which is always a good idea).

The tricky part about keeping multiple calendars is dealing with conflicts between the two. To see two calendars at a time, click the check box next to each calendar name in the navigation pane.

Superimpose Calendars

In Microsoft Outlook, viewing multiple calendars together is quite easy.

- Click the calendar in the navigation pane to open the calendar view.

- Select all the calendars that will appear together in the Navigation Pane.

Microsoft Outlook will then automatically display all checked calendars side by side.

Selecting Dates as a Group

When viewing a range of dates, it's not necessary to limit your view to specific days, weeks, or months. Let's say you would like to analyze a range of dates from September 25 through October 5.

- Click **September 25** in the To-Do bar, then (while holding down the Shift key)

- Click **October 5**, The entire period is selected and appears in the information viewer.

- The Date Navigator will appear once you click on the Folder pane.

- To test it, open **the calendar** that appears in the left corner.

Pin a Contact Card

The easiest way to view someone's contact information with the message you're reading (in the reading pane or its separate window) is to

- Right-click on **a person's email address**
- Choose "**Open Contact Card.**" An image of a pushpin is located in the upper-right corner of the contact card.
- Click **the pushpin**, the contact card will float on the screen
- Click **it again to make it disappear**.

Have you ever pinned a contact and it's no longer there? No worries. It's probably because Outlook is in its default full-screen mode. A full-screen Outlook screen hides the pinned contact when you click it off. Right-click on the Outlook screen and select Restore Down or Minimize. The contact should now appear.

CONCLUSION

With Outlook you'll get a feature-packed email client with a higher learning curve, but a lot more options to customize your email. Despite the fact that you may use Outlook every day, you might not know all of the cool things you can do with it.

Microsoft Outlook lets you send and receive an email, manage your calendar, store your contact information, and track your tasks. Most people think of Microsoft Outlook when it comes to email, but it has many other features that may be useful to you.

Download and install Outlook today and begin making the most of its features.

INDEX

"

"dialog boxes", 35
"discard" button, 67
"focused inbox", 1
"Run Now" button, 95
"ScreenTip", 35

A

A file, 16
A flag, 70
A note icon, 28
A screenshot, 80
A Tablet Computer, 271
ACME Corporation, 21
aggregation of attachments, 1
airplane mode, 4
Alerts dialog, 91, 94, 95
All Email Recipients, 279
an email client, 1
an incredibly versatile, 26
Anonymous groups, 132
Apple iOS, 1
archive data file, 108, 109
Archive data files, 108
Archive File text box, 108
Archiving for Posterity, 101
Area Codes, 278
Assigning tasks, 228
Attendee Availability page, 222
AutoArchive settings, 102, 104, 105
automatic download, 3, 196
automatic filtering, 96, 97

B

Back Ends, 49
BELLS AND WHISTLES, 159
Blocked Senders, 99, 100
box arrow, 56, 73, 75, 76
business cards, 34, 138, 256, 273

C

cable provider, 198
calendar events, 1
Calendar Location Box, 278
Calendar module, 146, 147, 149, 150, 151, 154, 155, 157, 258
Calendar views, 179
Calendar Wizardry, 41
CALENDAR'S POWER, 144
calendaring, 1, 274
Casanova's chauffeur, 144
checkmark, 71, 93, 94, 95, 158
cloud storage platforms, 1
clutter of email, 6
Cluttered inboxes, 9
color-code, 9
color-coding, 5
column's title, 131
Compact Navigation, 32
company" column, 131
complex business, 24
complimentary gift, 43
confirmation codes, 24
Contact Card, 286
contact management, 30

contact's middle initial, 127
conversations, 7, 111, 113, 114, 115, 117, 118

D

data gathering, 1
Date Navigator, 144, 145, 148, 285
Datebooks, 146
default fields, 22
default flag date, 72
Delegating authority, 230
Delivery Techniques, 10
desktop version, 1, 2, 243, 248, 252, 255, 260, 262
dialog box, 21, 22, 27, 32, 35, 47, 56, 67, 72, 73, 74, 75, 76, 79, 82, 85, 86, 87, 91, 92, 93, 94, 95, 96, 98, 100, 102, 103, 104, 106, 107, 116, 117, 120, 121, 122, 123, 124, 127, 129, 133, 134, 135, 141, 143, 145, 151, 153, 154, 156, 157, 167, 168, 171, 183, 187, 188, 191, 194, 195, 196, 204, 205, 206, 207, 208, 209, 211, 212, 213, 214, 215, 216, 217, 221, 226, 227, 230, 231, 233, 234, 235, 236, 237, 260, 262, 268
Dialog Box, 79, 268
dialog box title bar., 21
digital gadgets, 146
downward button., 60
Dropbox, 2, 31
Dropbox,, 2
Due Date box, 73, 161

E

E-Learning, 272
electronic equivalent, 24
Electronic gadgets, 146
electronic mail (email), 50
Email Account, 11
email box, 40
email client, 29, 201, 202, 286
email folder, 85, 97
Email Merging, 218
Email Provider, 198
Email Recipient, 265
emailing platforms, 1

F

Family Birthdays.", 25
Feed hyperlink, 194
File Dialog Box., 79
file format, 68
filter's sensitivity, 96
Filtering domains, 101
Filtering Junk Email, 95
financial institution, 63, 98
flagged items, 111
flagged messages, 71, 255
Flagging messages, 255
focus box, 9
Folder check box, 120
Folder pane, 31, 32, 65, 66, 85, 86, 89, 91, 108, 109, 158, 232, 236, 285
foreign languages, 99
Format Text tab, 53
free/busy schedule, 7
Front Ends, 49
full schedule, 159

G

G Suite, 1
geeky programmers, 276
general fields, 22
Gmail accounts., 4
Google calendar, 7
Google Workspace, 1, 2

H

hamburger button, 247, 249
handy flag, 73
handy flag means "Follow Up, 73
Home tab, 19, 23, 34, 35, 66, 74, 86, 95, 96, 100, 101, 115, 116, 118, 120, 121, 130, 132, 133, 136, 138, 140, 145, 179, 186, 215, 216, 220, 226, 267, 268
hotspot, 33
HTML files, 68

I

iCloud. Google, 2
icon title, 25
imaginary location, 86
Impact Charts, 283
inclusion of locations, 1
influx of junk, 95
information viewer, 33, 34, 285
instant flash, 36
Instant Search, 36
integrated waypoints, 2
interface, 29, 31, 176, 201, 252
internet browser, 130
internet connection, 5, 50, 254
Internet Explorer, 192, 193, 194, 195, 272
Internet link, 162
Internet provider, 198
Internet Service Provider, 49, 50
Internet service provider (ISP)., 198

J

jetsam, 84
journal jogging, 1
juggling work emails, 236
Junk Email Folder, 97
junkiest of junk, 97

L

label "mobile", 22
lawn mowings, 168
legitimate mail, 96, 97
lightbulb, 37
like Dropbox, Google Drive, 2
lunch dates, 147

M

magnification slider, 47
Mail Account Settings, 206
Mail button, 74, 75, 82, 197
Mail Merge Contacts dialogue box., 218
Mail module, 43, 52, 101, 104, 113, 116, 118, 120, 186, 226, 233
Mail Module, 58, 59, 60, 61, 63, 65, 67, 72, 73, 78, 85, 86, 89, 91, 96
Mailbird, 31
mailboxes, 1, 32, 59
Mailing Label Magic, 211

Mailing Labels, 212, 215
mailing list online, 99
management system software, 1
managing contacts, 1
Managing Recurring Tasks, 166
managing tasks, 1
Mark Joe, 21
Mastering Formal Letter Formalities, 218
Meeting Attendees, 278
meeting rooms, 6
Meetings Galore, 146
membership ID numbers, 24
memorable quotes., 24
merge template, 214
Microsoft, 1, 2, 6, 8, 10, 11, 16, 18, 20, 23, 29, 37, 42, 47, 49, 53, 57, 70, 75, 78, 111, 179, 193, 194, 199, 204, 212, 213, 216, 219, 229, 235, 236, 238, 240, 242, 251, 252, 257, 262, 266, 272, 274, 275, 277, 278, 280, 285, 286
Microsoft Exchange, 1, 29, 42, 49, 57, 219, 235, 236, 238, 262, 274
Microsoft Exchange Server, 1, 29, 49, 57, 219, 238
Microsoft suite., 1
Microsoft Visual, 1
Microsoft Visual Studio, 1
MICROSOFT WORD, 211
Microsoft's Office, 199
Mobile Calendar, 248
modern messenger environment, 31
modern standards, 31
multi-functional program, 31
multinational corporations, 199

Multiple Calendars, 157
MULTIPLE EMAIL ACCOUNTS, 198
multi-user software, 1

N

Nagging by Flagging, 70
Navigation Bar, 194, 228
navigation pane, 67, 87, 102, 106, 197, 230, 231, 260, 275, 284, 285
Navigation pane, 108, 116, 144
navigation window, 74, 75, 77, 82
new task box, 23
Notes pane, 22
note-taking, 1

O

Office packages, 1
Off-topic discussions, 114
OneDrive, 2, 16, 251, 264, 275
one-time Mozilla, 29
Online Backup, 273
Organizing Folders, 84
original state-Schedule, 246
Outlook 97 version 8.0, 2
Outlook Mobile, 1, 2, 243

P

personal data, 63, 238
personal information manager, 29
personal resource, 1
phishing, 62, 63, 98
plane, 4
platforms, 1, 2, 5, 6, 242

playing podcasts, 192
Podcasts, 192, 196
Postbox, 29, 30
potential match, 10
preference folder, 86
professional communication, 49
projectors, 6
public folders, 262
public library, 262
public policy, 190

Q

Quick Access, 54, 176, 177, 267, 281, 282
Quick Access Toolbar, 54, 176, 177, 267, 281, 282
Quick-Step templates, 121, 122

R

radio stations', 192
Reading Feeds, 197
reading pane, 12, 43, 45, 47, 48, 58, 59, 60, 61, 63, 89, 90, 109, 113, 253, 254, 286
Reading Pane, 59, 89, 277
recurring task, 166, 167, 169
regenerating task, 168, 169
Regenerating Tasks, 168
Reminder checkbox, 74, 161, 165
Rename Category, 27
Ribbon, 23, 34, 35, 59, 66, 67, 72, 74, 77, 78, 82, 85, 86, 91, 95, 96, 100, 101, 104, 114, 116, 118, 124, 129, 130, 131, 136, 138, 139, 140, 145, 147, 151, 155, 157, 164, 166, 168, 170, 171, 174, 177, 178, 179, 183, 211, 213, 215, 216, 220, 223, 226, 254, 255, 256, 282, 283
row-and-column format, 178, 180
RSS Feed folder, 194
Run Rules Now icon, 95

S

Safe Senders lists, 97, 100
satellite provider, 198
Scheduling appointments, 146
scheduling assistant, 10
Scheduling meetings, 6
Screen Tips, 35
ScreenTip, 35
Secure Password Authentication, 203
share dialog box, 16, 18, 78, 266
signature button, 82
Simple Listview, 164, 172
Simple Mail Transfer Protocol, 203
single click, 31, 72, 118
Skype, 240, 253, 264, 273, 274, 279
Skype conversation, 253
slicing and dicing, 20
slightest glance, 5
Smart Art, 282
Smartphones, 271
snooze button, 74
Social Media Basics, 191
SOCIAL MEDIA MAGIC, 190
software, 1, 29, 30, 31, 96, 240
Sorting Items, 182
spam messages, 99
Spike, 30, 31
stand-alone application, 1

Start Date box, 73, 161
sticky notes, 24
Subject text box, 79
Superimpose Calendars, 285

T

Tags group, 72
Taking Peeks, 36
Tallying votes, 227
Tasks Module, 159
Team platform, 2
teamwork, 31, 219
telephone provider, 198
Tentative, 223, 224
text box, 45, 52, 64, 67, 77, 83, 85, 93, 104, 105, 108, 118, 121, 127, 128, 129, 139, 146, 149, 152, 162, 165, 214, 229, 237, 266
Text box, 73
textbox, 37, 53, 64
The archive file, 108
The blank label document, 214
The Date box, 145
The flag icon, 248
The folder pane, 31, 32
the influx of flotsam, 84
The junk email feature, 98
The large mail folder, 88
the Mail Server, 207
the navigation bar, 19, 23, 34, 36, 41, 42, 43, 44, 45, 197, 211, 216, 225, 229
the ribbon, 12, 20, 21, 34, 35, 58, 75, 78, 81, 86, 90, 137, 160, 169, 177, 178, 213, 229, 253, 264, 273
The Rules Wizard, 84, 91, 93

Thunderbird, 29, 30
Time management, 20
tiny pop-up window, 36
To-Do bar, 34, 71, 145, 169, 173, 174, 285
To-Do Bar, 34, 173, 174
TO-DO bar, 71
toggle, 9, 22
trackball, 39
transferring junk mail, 9
True Dark Mode, 3
two identical inboxes, 9

U

Unified Inbox, 276
Urging merger, 211

V

View Sorting, 131
voting buttons, 226, 227
voting feature, 226

W

Web App, 262, 263
web browsing, 1
Web Email Basics, 253
Web Page Address, 129
webpage, 57, 129
website passwords, 24
Windows Phone devices, 1
Word document, 78
Word Document, 18, 266
word processor, 53
Word window, 16, 18
Word's Mail Merge, 211

Workspace Expansion, 45
workweek button, 34
wrong calendar., 8

Z

zip code, 22
zoom percentage, 47

Made in the USA
Coppell, TX
26 May 2022